# SQUISHED:

*Jackie Kennedy,*

*Espionage,*

*Murder and Me*

By:
Philip E. Myers

*"You're going to end up squished in a trash can somewhere."*

*Jacqueline Kennedy Onassis to the author, January 8, 1992*

**Visit:**
**Facebook.com/philmyersauthor**
**or**
**www.philmyersauthor.com**

See which of a dozen more books by Myers have been released, all described at the end of this book

# TABLE OF CONTENTS

*"You're going to end up squished in a trash can somewhere."*

*Jacqueline Kennedy Onassis to the author, January 8, 1992*

## PROLOGUE: BOLTS OUT OF THE BLUE

There's an odd closeness that develops when someone involves you in the quest to solve the murder of a loved one. Jacqueline Bouvier Kennedy Onassis told me she loved the spymaster, Leonid Tarassuk, after he moved to New York from Leningrad in the early 1970's. And to our mutual surprise the investigation of his murder linked it to the murder of her husband, the President.

One sunny Fall afternoon in 1992, I found myself sitting in the library of her apartment at 1040 Fifth Avenue in New York watching her share memories of a murdered Russian who spied for the US with his best friend, a Russian nuclear physicist who was also part of the spy group. Both of them, Gulia who was sitting across from me that afternoon, and Jackie, had loved Leonid. Gulia and Leonid had been best friends in college in Leningrad. Jackie and the murdered spymaster had been intensely close after he went to work at the Metropolitan Museum of Art in the early 70's, about a decade after the JFK assassination and shortly after the death of Aristotle Onassis, her second husband. Leonid was her primary collaborator on the book she edited about an exhibit at the Met, *In the Russian Style*. And their friendship had continued. When he wasn't making trips back to the Soviet Union on a fake passport, to buy arms for Iraq from Russia, he was stopping by her apartment on his way home from work.

When the surviving Russian spy, Gulia, first told me the story of the 1950's plot to warn the US of a Soviet nuclear first strike there was no suggestion that Leonid had been murdered. He died in a car crash in 1990 in France. It was Jackie who introduced the idea of the murder to our project. And everything, thereafter, in our research, including psychics we'd consulted, indicated that she had been right. At that point we didn't know who ordered the hit or how far the story went. Jackie and I were sure there was still something very large we hadn't uncovered. And it proved to be right; the research ultimately would uncover a likely Soviet mole high in the US government who had served as Chairman of the Democratic Party and apparently had two murders on his hands.

The afternoon in her apartment had something of the feel of a wake, albeit a very small and private one.  For once, in Jackie's presence, her piercing eyes were focused on someone else. I was able to look around the room, as I hadn't previously, to see the family pictures, her copy of JFK's Pulitzer Prize winning "Profiles in Courage" on the shelf beside me and the snapshots of the grandkids that were scotch-taped to a mirror.  It was an incredibly intimate experience.

When it began to be apparent that the story we were researching, Gulia and Leonid's story, touched on the JFK assassination I thought she would bail out of our book research project.  But she didn't. She was fearless. She was free. She was very, very smart.

It took me a while to figure out how my life was similar to that of the former First Lady. She had been married to a President and later to the richest man in the world.  I was a Methodist preacher's son from small-town Pennsylvania.  On the face of it we were not two peas in a pod.  And yet we were.

The JFK assassination had been a bolt out of the blue. It shaped and colored the rest of her life and how people reacted to her. My bolt out of the blue was a hidden tale of Cold War espionage that fell on me without warning while I was in the Soviet Union on business. Suddenly I knew spies. Suddenly I was in the middle of the hunt for a Soviet mole in the U.S. government. And suddenly I was researching the murder of Leonid, the spymaster, with the woman who had been his intimate friend.

He and Leonid had wanted to save the world from the insanity of a nuclear first strike.

*SQUISHED* is the story of how our bolts from the blue tied us together. And ultimately it is the story about who made those two murders happen.

# Chapter 1

## *Random Waves of Mystery: Antibes, France 2006*

Jackie had been gone for twelve years that day I sat at lunch in the south of France, trying to decide how to tell our story at last. As I sat on a seaside terrace in the restaurant of a five-star hotel, I found it in the waves I spotted in the Mediterranean. The odd waves came from nowhere. No boats had swept by leaving a wake. They were much too isolated to be a Tsunami, too small to be a serious threat. I doubt they were more than a football field's length across; hardly the stuff of terror. But clearly, they were big enough not to be the normal variation in the surface of a sparkling blue Med. The sailor in me knew that an inattentive skipper's small boat could be swamped and capsized if it took them broadside. But there were no boats to lose, no swabbies to save, not even a swimmer to absorb a mouthful of salt water.

The threat was there but nothing was threatened. It reminded me of that day in 1991 when the first knowledge of the spy plot fell on my head during the first of my 58 trips to Russia.

The calm sea was wasting its odd little tantrum on the floating swimming platforms moored offshore from the hotel pool and dock. Any swimmer sunbathing on the platforms with eyes closed would surely have been dumped suddenly and unexpectedly into the salty brine, incensed at the nasty joke Neptune (or some playful lover) had devised. But there was not even a floating sunbather to disturb. I doubt anyone else even noticed the set of about six waves. They made me sit up, however, in wonderment, and take a pause in sipping my favorite aperitif, red Dubonnet. For one brief instant, something in my brain registered DANGER, just as it did that day the spy first confided in me in 1991. But it was simply a primitive reflex. In my corner table perched over the sea it would take a wave at least 50 feet higher to even splash me. But I made the calculation just to be sure.

This was no waterpark with false waves made for the kids to be pretend surfers. This was a mystery of nature slipping unexpectedly into my consciousness, turning my brain on despite the point of my indulgent seaside lunch with the rare glass of wine being to allow myself to disengage, to clear my mind and organize a complicated tale of murder and espionage. I sought to escape for a few precious hours and renew myself. I reveled in the warm weather, the California-like blue sky.

It was almost as good as being back home in Santa Barbara.

Neptune seemed to be making his point to me alone, just as the spy had.

My mind slipped from sinking ships and danger avoidance to the equally odd passage in the biography of movie goddess Jane Fonda that I had just read. She had been practically at this very spot with another movie goddess of a prior generation. Jane Fonda wrote she was astonished when Greta Garbo invited her for a swim when they were together at Fonda's father's rented villa. Garbo led her to the cove, dropped her robe and dove naked into the Mediterranean. Perhaps the local coves simply decided thereafter to have their waters be more shapely and mysterious evermore. I rather liked that explanation of my mysterious waves. Water with a memory! The Russians and Japanese were actually researching that sort of thing.

My mind suddenly put Jane Fonda and Greta Garbo on those floating docks. The scene in "On Golden Pond" where a stunning forty-something Fonda in a bikini does a backflip off a dock played perfectly here. Add Garbo sunbathing in the buff and being tossed off the dock and I had the perfect synthesis of realities and film fantasies blended with a confusion of times. Mixing them all up you have a strange reality, but maybe a complete truth. It was all very French, very much like the writings of Alain Robbe-Grillet, one of my favorites, who makes the sequence of events impossible to figure out. Very appropriate for an espionage lunch in a French paradise.

This slippery notion of truth and reality led me to almost lie to the movie-star handsome waiter, Jerome, and tell him Jackie had recommended the restaurant to me. I liked Jerome. He reminded me of Jackie's butler from 14 years earlier, the first time I went to her penthouse. In his starched white coat (like the butler's) Jerome was the antithesis of the random maritime confusion below. Maybe his very big sunglasses made me think of Jackie. She was iconic in the feminine version of big sunglasses.

I decided not to lie, but to stay with the immediate reality.

Jackie had given me plenty of advice when I first came across the spy story, but none of it about restaurants. So, I merely chatted with Jerome, who had precious little else to do thanks to a slow day and a small crowd. No doubt he was selected partly for his looks, in a breathtaking setting where anything short of perfection would seem incongruous. It was Jerome's first day on the job. He acknowledged that snagging a position at the Hotel Du Cap Eden Roc's seaside restaurant was a notable coup. He had seven years' experience at a chi-chi Monaco beachside club first. But Monaco was so stuffy. Now he lived and frolicked in the oh-so-cool and more untidy adjacent village of Juan-les-Pins. And he had been entrusted with the care of four of the most glorious lunch tables in Christendom. His title was "Chef de Rang" (Chief of a Group of Four tables). I figured this was every bit as good as my title of Chief Executive Officer of Typhoon Security Technology. That afternoon he was probably doing a better job of fighting entropy and maintaining order than was I.

Jerome's domain was part of the Hotel du Cap-Eden-Roc in Antibes, on the Mediterranean. Looking more like a king's chateau than a hotel open to the public, this place was the backdrop that F. Scott Fitzgerald used for *Tender is the Night*. This was where an endless succession of the rich and famous gather for lunches full of structure and perfection. The hills of the Azure Coast as it bends around look like a painter's imagined paradise. But it is real. The infinity pool transcends its recreational purpose and becomes a meditation in stone and water, providing calm and health and heated comfort that properly mimic the perfect sea and mountains. Man might not be God, but at least he could control the pool temperature and do a damn good job of simulating the Almighty's perfection. (And, if you're not staying at the hotel you can have a dip in the pool for only $75 per day at that point!! Paradise can be bought.)

And yet I'd felt that hint of danger out of the blue.

Jerome was responsible for maintaining order in a local system surrounded by the unnoticed threat of random mini-tsunamis. He bore his responsibility well. Since it was his first day on the job, his first lunch ever at the Eden-Roc, as well as my own, I decided we would be forever bonded together. He laughed and enjoyed the concept. At that point, I figured I probably needed to hire him for my company and handed him a business card. It was definitely appropriate to hire someone who could manage to maintain order and civility at those particular four tables. I imagined that he would understand what my work with chaos was like. He could undoubtedly apply his skills to the oddities of my world. Struggle is struggle; good execution is good execution.

He seemed a little surprised when I answered his question of just what exactly my company did and what sort assistance I might need.  I doubt he thought of himself as a counter-terrorist. But I thought it suited him fine, just as I had learned it suited me. I'll have to explain later why his skills were so transferable. It would have helped if someone had given me that talk fifteen years ago.

## Chapter 2

### *Car Crashes and Waves of Death, 1964 and 1990*

On July 5, 1964, a twenty-six-year-old French lad and his sixteen-year-old fiancée puttered along in his Volvo on a French country road, not expecting to be murdered. For them there was no hint of danger. It happened quickly and without warning, just a short quick slide straight into a tree. French military security was quite efficient in edging their car off the highway using a larger truck. It looked like an accident of driving. But it was an accident of identification. The murder was intentional for sure, although the French government would not admit it for about thirty-five more years.

The French intelligence services were looking for an Algerian exile's Volvo and intended to murder him. Apparently, they thought he was part of a plot to assassinate President DeGaulle, and it was just a few months after the assassination of JFK. Instead, they screwed up on the little detail of the license plate number, and murdered Jean-Claude Saint-Aubin and his young bride-to-be.

Twenty-six years later, another car went off a French road killing Jackie's friend Leonid and his wife. It was another murder. But this time (after how much practice, one can only speculate) the 1990 murder by staged automobile accident on a French roadway worked out as intended. This time there were a couple of extra deaths, "collateral damage," but at least the right person was murdered. This time the murder victim was an intimate friend of Jacqueline Kennedy Onassis. She was the first one to suggest to me he had been murdered.

The "collateral damage" was Lucy Carter, age sixty, and her husband John, age sixty-four, an electrical engineer. They had packed up their little grey Citroen in front of their working-class home in Abbey Wood, London for a September holiday in France. They travelled fairly light, with just one suitcase, her makeup case and a few other small bags. Lucy took both her long silver chain necklace and the short gold one according to the police report.

The boxy little Citroen was far from a sports car, but John could imagine more as he wore the "Corvette" emblem watch he liked so much. In his wallet was just one credit card, from Midland Bank, but two checkbooks, his Eurocheck checkbook from Midland Bank, and another checkbook from Société Générale, a French bank. For writing checks he had his good silver pen. Lucy took her chestnut and black purse and the coordinated chestnut sack.

Although they were off to France, Lucy carried her London Transport pass. Lucy's passport, number 910403, had only a few months of validity left. She would need a new one before next year's holiday. His passport, number 350471, had almost ten more years to run. Their auto insurance with Lloyds was paid up through December. Everything was in order, so they said their goodbyes to John's brother, Stanley, who lived in the neighborhood, and they were off.

Across the Channel, Brittany was their goal. Although officially French, the natives of Brittany are of Celtic stock and think of the French almost as foreigners. They resent the lure of Paris that induces so many of their young to go there seeking their futures. They have a separate language, Breton, and come from the same genetic stock as the Welsh. The Bretons have more of a sense of mysticism than the highly rational French. The bleak, almost surreal countryside, swept by constant ocean winds for centuries, has electric-green grass suggesting something very odd in the soil, and in the wind. The locals like their superstitions, which are plentiful.

The western-most point of France is a rugged promontory in Brittany, the Pointe du Raz, which attracts tourists for its almost mystical beauty. Seafarers, however, are not so taken with it. The adjacent "Bay of the Dead" is aptly named for the many victims of shipwreck that have sloshed about in its waters.

The quaint old town of Quimper a few miles away is the jumping off point for visitors on their way to the Bay of the Dead. In Quimper Breton ladies sometimes still wear lace headdresses just as they did hundreds of years ago. You barely focus on the giant nuclear reactors at Plogoff, a few kilometers down the road towards the beach at Audierne. Quimper could almost be a medieval city frozen in time.

Years ago, when I was a student in France, I took a train to Quimper, a bus to Audierne, and hiked to the Bay of the Dead. There I spent a blustery November night as the only guest in a hotel at the Bay of the Dead. That night the soccer club of Plogoff held its annual ball at the hotel, and I got invited to join in by the band, which had provided the only other diners in the hotel restaurant earlier that evening. Alas, because I was a stranger, none of the girls from the little Breton village would dance with me. So, I sat and watched, figuring this was certainly the last I would ever have to do with Quimper and the Bay of the Dead.

But John and Lucy Carter were on their way to Quimper, and so was my destiny.

September 11, 1990 was clear and dry, a perfect vacation day; the autumn bad weather had not yet set in near the coast.  Just outside Quimper, on the straight, flat Avenue de Morbihan, John first saw Leonid's black Ford Escort with Belgian plates coming towards him when it moved out to pass a car. Although it was coming straight at him, it appeared to have plenty of room to move back to its own side. Zipping along at about a hundred and twenty km/hr, it quickly bypassed the car it was overtaking which was going only eighty or ninety km/hr. About a hundred meters past the slowpoke, it started its return to its own side.  All seemed perfectly fine.

But the Escort suddenly started to swerve every which way. It was evident that the driver had lost control.  First the Escort veered off to its right into the guardrail, scraping along, leaving black paint as Leonid frantically tried to brake. Suddenly it lunged out of the guardrail, across its own lane and back into John's.  For twenty-five feet John managed to leave skid marks before the Escort slammed directly into the driver's side at the front, the very worst possible angle of collision. The roof of his Citroen was torn off by the impact; the front of the car was totally gone. John was dead instantly. While traffic backed up in both directions, the road was closed and the doctor with the ambulance drew his blood. There was no alcohol in it.

Lucy, gravely injured, went to Laennec Hospital where she died a short time later. Police photographers captured the scene, and the authorities interviewed the one witness, the driver of the car overtaken. The wreckage was hauled off to the Maigne garage in Quimper.

The police report laid all the blame for the accident on the driver of the black Escort, Leonid. Curiously John's family took no steps to make any claim against Leonid's insurance or his estate. Thirteen years later the neighbors back in Abbey Wood had almost all moved, and virtually no one remembered John and Lucy Carter. Everyone thought that September 11, 1990 had been John and Lucy's exit from the scene of life. But now everyone will know about them, for the police report of the 1990 deaths would appear to be as much a whitewash of a murder as was the original police report on the 1964 staged "accident." Too many indications make clear that Leonid was murdered.  Whether his car was tampered with, or the police report falsified, or the police conveniently did not look for signs of car tampering, Jackie went to her grave convinced her friend had been murdered. The psychic she consulted agreed.

Leonid and his wife loved to escape Manhattan for his country house in the hills of Eastern Pennsylvania.  It was very typically Russian to have a country "dacha," no matter how modest. Even though he had been in Manhattan for nearly 20 years, some elements of his Russianness remained.  He planned to retire there, but for the moment his cousin, Israel, a friend since boyhood in Odessa, was living in the Pennsylvania house. At the end of August Leonid's best friend and college fencing partner, Gulia, (my nickname for this eminent man who shall be known herein only by his nickname) had hoped to spend a week at the Pennsylvania dacha seeing his old friend. Gulia was coming from Leningrad to spend six months as a visiting professor at Stanford's Center for International Security and Arms Control ("CISAC"). There he would hobnob with Bill Perry who became U.S. Secretary of Defense, and Condi Rice, who became U.S. Secretary of State.  He hoped for a repeat of his previous reunion in New York with Leonid, when they spoke about the old days of fencing at University together in Leningrad, of committing treason together, of saving the world together, while getting "pretty drunk and happy."

But this time Gulia's visa was delayed, and he had to overfly New York and go straight to California.  Before setting off on their annual trek to Europe, Leonid and his wife, Nina, went out to their country house in Pennsylvania where they wrote their wills. Nina complained to her daughter, Irina that she was never going to get to see her grandchildren.  Irina wished her mother would quit bugging her to get pregnant. She was newly married and enjoying being childless. And little brother Ilya was just finishing high school. He certainly shouldn't be providing grandchildren yet.

Leonid and Nina flew first to Scotland, sending post cards home to the children. From there they flew to Brussels where they rented a black Ford Escort for the drive to France. They'd be seeing some old friends at a convention of antique arms.

And then they were dead.

And Gulia was terrified that he'd be next one of the traitors against the Soviet Union to get liquidated.

## Chapter 3

### *Would You Like To Buy A Nuclear Submarine?*

New York to me will always be two places in the sky:  the UN Plaza Hotel pool and Jackie's penthouse where Leonid had been a regular visitor. They are perfect perches for observing life, just like the lunch terrace at the Hotel du Cap-Eden-Roc.

Pools keep showing up in this story. A good part of my reason for having lunch at the Hotel du Cap-Eden-Roc, where I saw my random waves of mystery, was to check out the hotel's pool. Frankly, but for the regular swimming over the last 30 years, I would probably have short-circuited long ago. Paradoxically, being in the water keeps me grounded. The cardiovascular elevation as I pump out those laps dissipates the stress, clears the mind, and helps me make sense of the craziness of life.

If you want to swim in the sky in New York the UN Plaza Hotel fits the bill perfectly. Its pool is in the middle of a skyscraper, at the 27th floor.  Turn your head to take a breath during a lap and you catch a glimpse of blue sky. Do a flip turn and watch Manhattan invert.

Uptown from the UN Plaza, about twenty blocks on the Upper East in Manhattan is the Council on Foreign Relations. A former oil baron's mansion, when you walk in it's still obvious that this is where power and money live. The marble, the chandeliers, the curving staircase and the wood-panelled living room-turned-conference-room for up to 80 people: the place screams that it's a citadel of the 1%, the people who "matter."

Now it is a think tank par excellence. And it is a swell place for conspiracies. Kissinger, Rockefeller, and a tabloid-full of household names come and go from its elegant mansion-turned-headquarters at Park and 68th in Manhattan. Maurice Templesman, Mrs. Onassis's live-in friend for the last years of her life, was a member.

And in 1990 the Council had a branch in Santa Barbara, where as a director myself I enjoyed the regular dinner meetings with diplomats and experts who came through town.

Every spring the Council would sponsor a two-day conference in New York on a current hot topic in international relations. We provincials were invited to come for a bit of enlightenment. The 1990 meeting topic was "Glasnost and Perestroika," (meaning openness and restructuring): What's up in Gorbachev's Soviet Union.

Gorbachev was the new Soviet premier, and a reformer. He was trying hard to get the Soviet economy to come back to life. Shops were empty at the time. Food was scare. And Gorbachev was increasingly hated by the old Communist party hard-liners who blamed him for making things worse. Yet America and the West celebrated his rise to power. He was seen as a hopeful figure who promoted peace and cooperation and was not afraid to make friends of Western governments.

About sixty of us from around the country gathered to hear a panel discuss Gorbachev's reforms. The panel included General Lee Butler, head of strategic planning for the Joint Chiefs of Staff and number two to General Colin Powell. The session was moderated by ABC news anchor and former Nixon aide Diane Sawyer, a luminous presence. Sitting a few feet from her for two days was a great delight as she lived up to her billing of being both beautiful and tremendously bright.

Gorbachev was in Washington that week and two members of his summit entourage came to brainstorm with us. One was Serge

Mikoyan, whose father had been the second-in-command to Soviet premier Khrushchev at the height of the Cold War. Serge was a survivor of a different era and looked it. Badly dressed and glum, he dutifully described this year's Soviet Communist party line of reform. I had the feeling that if next year's party line was "let's shoot all the Ukrainians," he'd be on board.

However, Vlad Zubock, travelling with Mikoyan, was a different matter. Early 30's, fresh-faced, articulate and well-dressed, he wore a fashionable sports jacket of Italian raw silk, and virtually babbled perfect English. At a break, he explained that he was Gorbachev's analyst of American venture capital. I was astonished Gorbachev had someone looking into whether Silicon Valley could be replicated outside Moscow.

Vlad was going with Gorbachev in a couple of days to Silicon Valley, heart of Venture Capitalist country. Yet Vlad groused that he had no meetings set up with venture capitalists. I was quite surprised and volunteered to see if I could arrange something through my old Stanford buddies who were still working in the tech world there. During the lunch break I made a few calls. Presto digito, Vlad had a tour of Hewlett-Packard World Headquarters which happens to be on the Stanford campus. Just down the road is the heart of the venture capital community where one of my best friends worked. To Vlad I was a magician. He just didn't understand how an open society works. If you want to talk to someone, just pick up the phone and call! If you want to meet someone, ask him. No one gets shot for being ambitious and audacious.

Back in the Soviet Union you had to apply for permission for everything. It was the whole legal foundation of things for over 70 years. Every action not specifically permitted was prohibited. Goodness, that single legal fact would be enough to kill the entire venture capital industry, something the Russians then didn't understand. American venture capital is entirely premised on upsetting established ways of doing things with "disruptive technology." Think of it as goal-directed techie tsunamis intended to wash away the old.

So, after my phone calls to set up meetings, Vlad went off to Stanford and had a dandy time. Stanford University invited him to return for six months. He would brainstorm at the Center for International Security and Arms Control (CISAC), headed by Bill Perry who would soon be Clinton's Secretary of Defense. The mission that Winter and Spring of 1991-92 for Vlad and the CISAC folks was to think what to do with the brainpower and technology locked up in the Soviet military sector. They needed to be "converted" to civilian, money-making productive uses. Gorbachev was on the right track that there was exciting technology locked up in the military. But he had very little idea how to move that technology into private startup companies.

CISAC also had the good sense to invite Vlad's mentor, Gulia, a nuclear physicist, to come to Stanford for an overlapping six-month session. After all, who better knew the ins and outs of science and technology in the military sector than a member of the nuclear priesthood who had a key role in creating the hydrogen bomb!

Gulia was then in his 60's yet retained almost an impish smile and energy. His spirit was young. His intensity was uncompromised by age. This was an exciting man to meet. This was someone who had had a key role in giving the Soviet Union the hydrogen bomb and the power to destroy the world. And he played the violin with humor and passion. Now he was relishing having a role in converting swords into ploughshares. Now he wanted to have a role in saving the world, not destroying it.

Another of the regular participants in the CISAC sessions was a young Russia expert, an unlikely position perhaps for a Black woman. But Condoleezza Rice was not a person who knew limits. She was a one-woman sociological tsunami. Condi came from a modest southern background and became a superstar. She played piano, figure-skated, spoke Russian, attracted the attention of the first President Bush and became his National Security Advisor. And eventually she was to become Secretary of State.

Gulia was distributing a working paper at CISAC on business opportunities in defense conversion in the Soviet Union. Alas, he was having no luck enticing venture capitalists, crony capitalists, big corporate capitalists, or even bankrupt capitalists into taking business in the Soviet Union seriously.

Vlad sat at my dining room table in Santa Barbara having tea and cookies one evening. He asked if I would take a look at Gulia's working paper to see if any of the defense conversion projects seemed promising.

To be honest, the working paper gave me one of the best laughs I had had in years. Later in my office that evening, I literally fell out of my chair laughing at the idea of turning "Typhoon" class nuclear submarines into

Caribbean cruise ships. It was beyond conception that hundreds of tourists would confine themselves for a week in an 800-foot long, double-hulled titanium submarine with nuclear reactors of dubious reputation. Where would the pool be? How about the ocean-view bar? OK, maybe there was a gym. But Houston, we had a problem. A big problem!

It turns out that Typhoon subs are so big they actually do have a plunge pool. Still, I tried to gently let Vlad down and ask what else he had. But then, my wife stunned us both by jumping into the conversation with the amazing assertion that they could be oil drill ships under the polar ice pack.

Now, if this option might not occur to your spouse, let me note that Phyllis was trained as an oil industry engineer. And in another of those crazy flukes in life, she had just finished a project to analyze what kind of oil drill rigs could operate in conditions of extreme polar ice flows. She had degrees from Columbia and MIT in structural engineering and had worked for Exxon and Chevron designing platforms. And she had just finished a study that concluded that only submarine drillships (which did not exist), could be used in extreme ice environments. Otherwise the ice would simply wipe away the platforms, or artificial islands, or any other perches for drills to the seafloor.   But if the sub were under the ice, it could drill safely.

Vlad asked if she could put together any details so he could explain the concept. Clearly, he was loving it!  In a few days, she knocked together a briefing paper on the case for submarine drillships. And soon I had an invitation to go to the Soviet Union with the paper and meet the most senior folks in the submarine world and Russian Duma (parliament) to talk about taking over their Typhoon submarine fleet.

Perhaps, I figured, this would seem a bit odd to folks in the CIA or NSA or whatever agency kept track of Russian submarines. What the heck was a Santa Barbara lawyer more accustomed to wills and trusts doing with an offer from the Soviets to buy six nuclear attack subs for $60 million apiece.

Methinks at that point I started to show up on the radar screen in Langley, Virginia– CIA headquarters. Would I look like a rogue arms dealer? Good grief, how would I explain to anyone that I was just a hometown lawyer with an abiding curiosity who was looking for an interesting business project? I had never had my own nuclear attack sub before. But gee, it did sound like fun I guess. At least I knew where to get one (well, make that six actually)!  The fact that the Russians were going through me to deal with their fleet of Typhoons was really approaching the absurd.  But it was happening nonetheless.  Amazing what can happen when you just open your mouth and offer to set up a meeting with a venture capitalist.

The first time that Jackie heard the Typhoon submarine story she compared me to a Woody Allen character stumbling his way through nuclear war. I had taken some exception to the notion at first, but with time I have concluded that she exactly captured from day one the farcical aspects of it.  She was one smart editor.  And at first, I missed that we were characters in the same story.  But I think she knew right away.

For it was my guy, Gulia, dealing with the subs amidst his concerns about getting liquidated, who was the best friend of her dear friend, Leonid, who had died in the car crash.

Jackie and I had become oddly connected.

## Chapter 4

### *Preparing for the Evil Empire*

After Vlad's visit to my home in Santa
Barbara he urged me to go to Stanford to
meet Gulia in November 1990. They were
both due to return to the USSR shortly and if
anything was to come of the Typhoon
submarine idea I needed to meet the man.
Vlad explained that both of them had been
looking at ideas of how to restructure the US-
USSR military relationship away from
confrontation to cooperation. And mind you,
this was before the collapse of the Soviet
Union, so very remarkable and a good lesson
of what can go on quietly under the radar.

Vlad also wanted to talk to more venture
capitalists and asked me to set up something.
I contacted an old dorm buddy, Keith Geeslin,
who was with Sprout Group, venture
capitalists, who offered to talk to some of his
pals in the clubby venture capital world and
set up a lunch for us. Keith called me back
with discouraging news. The buzz in the
community was that Russian deals weren't
worth the trouble; they were too time
consuming. Only one Silicon Valley VC deal
with Russia had closed, in biotech. In that

single case, someone doing his homework about a startup in the Valley had discovered scientific papers on the key technology from a Russian institute. So, he had gone over to try to get them to participate. The effort had nearly totally consumed him for 18 months. In that time, a VC partner ought to have been working on five to eight deals. Thus, his partners were not happy, and a Russian deal had become a hard sell, good technology or not.

Keith suggested to Vlad and me, however, that computer programming might work. He was aware that some Indians who attended Stanford went home and convinced the Indian government to support developing programming for US companies as an export industry. Maybe Russia could be an alternative.

I went to meet Gulia who loved the idea immediately. He was going home in a couple days and volunteered to look for a programming group we might start with.

Gulia was extremely nervous, however, about the political situation back home. Gorbachev had recently appointed several hardline pro-Communists to key positions. It was possible that the reforms might come to a screeching halt. He went so far as to suggest he might get melted down for the gold in his teeth and he didn't seem to be kidding. The hardliners didn't like reformers like him!

Once he was back in Leningrad (the name hadn't yet changed back to St. Petersburg) he got busy. Soon he was telling me he'd found just the right group at the Politechnic University, roughly equivalent to Cal-Tech or MIT.

I got a formal invitation to visit in June 1991, which was necessary for a business visa. It included his offer that once I hit the border I wouldn't be allowed to pay for anything; I'd be a guest of an agency of the Soviet Union devoted to defense conversion (ARCTIS, or the Agency for Research Cooperation and Technical Innovation Support). Gulia was its boss.

I had enough frequent flyer miles on Pan Am to get me in first class to Helsinki, Finland, a hop, skip and a jump from Leningrad. The night I spent there in luxury at the Intercontinental Hotel was like a last night in civilization before being blasted into space. I was about to enter a whole new world in ways I couldn't begin to imagine.

## Chapter 5

### *Welcome To The Evil Empire: Leningrad, June 1991*

The absolutely rotten road that threatened our absolutely rotten car told me Gulia was right about Russia's rotten condition. Much of the pavement had been scraped off in anticipation of repaving. In the States, a road in such condition routinely would be closed until the repaving was finished. Here no one seemed the slightest bit surprised to have cars directed over a lava-flow of ruts and drops that easily could crunch the bottom of the car. What should have been the simple orderliness of a level road had been converted into an asphalt obstacle course.

The car was about as bad as the road. His "Lada" was a Soviet version of a boxy little 1968 Fiat. Gulia's had 78,000 kilometers on the odometer and was charitably described as an old heap. It had a stick shift, carburetor instead of fuel injection, no radio and looked to be on the verge of having all parts shake off. The nubby, garish upholstery was an odd red pattern, almost a brocade. It looked like the curtains at Grandma's house. Yet it was wildly unusual for a Soviet to have a private car; it might as well have been a Bentley.

Gulia traveled with a gas can in the trunk, which is horribly dangerous, of course. He couldn't leave too much gas in the tank because of the risk thieves would siphon it off. We passed mile-long gas lines with waits over an hour, so it was clear why the thieves operate. One day we noticed an odd bulge in the front right tire. He explained that to obtain a new tire was difficult and expensive, costing ten days' wages. He would have to start by posting a sign near a garage and waiting for a call from a black marketeer. At one point, going the official, legal way of applying to the state store, he had waited ten years for a set of tires!

Welcome to the Russian roulette of consumer survival under the Soviets!

All of the Soviet Union I had seen in my first three days there convinced me that the place was economically and spiritually bankrupt. The sheer shabbiness of it nearly had caused me to turn around and leave on my first day. Finding a baggage claim area at the airport illuminated by a single lightbulb dangling at the end of a 20-foot cord did not scream "high tech." The baggage carousel had a death rattle as it spun around.

I must be crazy, I thought, to consider starting up a business in computer programming here. The airport looked like Alcatraz 20 years after it had been abandoned. The whole city of Leningrad looked like Alcatraz 20 years after it had been abandoned. Everything was crumbling. At least banana republics manage a chaotic, happy charm. This place looked like it had been built by voodoo architects for zombies to inhabit.

How someone of Gulia's spark and brilliance had managed to survive was a mystery. Still, the very strong déja-vu experience I had on my first spin through downtown kept me from simply running to the airport and heading home. Something interesting was afoot, and I always pay attention to my non-rational experiences.

Vlad Zubock had introduced to me to Gulia, his mentor, in Palo Alto as a father of the Soviet hydrogen bomb program after World War II. Indeed, I later learned he personally had prepared the fuel for the first Soviet H-bomb in 1953 and loaded it on the truck to go to the test site.

Riding through that flat, green countryside on our way to the summer palace, Gulia and I were discussing the success of American "smart bombs" in the Persian Gulf

War.  As a Russian scientist, he was profoundly impressed at their ability to zero in on targets using lasers with television cameras recording it all. The battle for military supremacy was over, and he was clearly, if oddly, happy that the U.S. had won.  The photo of President Bush (the first one) plus the small American flag in his apartment made his pleasure a little more believable, and mysterious.

Gulia and I had taken the day off from business to visit the palaces of the Russian Czars at Pushkin and Pavlosk on the outskirts of Leningrad.  Actually, we had not much choice.  It was Election Day in Russia, and the palaces were about the only things open.  Since it was my first trip to Russia, they seemed like the perfect thing to explore.  That day, for the first time in a thousand years of nationhood, the Russian people elected a President.  Boris Yeltsin was triumphant. The Communist party, however, still ran the show. The botched coup d'état of 1991 was still two months in the future. The Soviet Union was still alive.  And treason against it still knew no statute of limitations.

Gulia pointed out where the German troops had encircled Leningrad in World War II while a million people in the city starved to death.  It was hard to imagine the snow and cold and death he associated with our pastoral outing. The perfection of the weather couldn't erase it for him or allow it to be real for me. I reveled in the warm weather, the California-like blue sky. It was almost as good as being back home in Santa Barbara, the same feeling I'd have 15 years later at the Hotel du Cap-Eden-Roc in Antibes.

Gulia's seven-year-old son, Siroja, bounced along in the back seat. He was enthralled by the apricots I had purchased at a farmers' market. There had been no bags to give out, and foolish me, I had gone shopping unprepared, without my own bag. But the old peasant woman with the tattered blue scarf on her hair had rustled up a newspaper. Her husband made a cone with the newspaper and put my kilo of apricots in it, delighted to have snared forty rubles (almost a week's wages) from a rich American. Gulia referred to the apricots as "gold." No one except seven-year-old Siroja seemed really comfortable devouring them with me. Siroja could still be turned into a happy consumer. He didn't know enough about deprivation to find American levels of consumption odd. Eating was just fun.

It was while Siroja was having fun in a playground in the country that the intrigue started.

## Chapter 6

### *Over The Edge With Nixon*

Out in that flat countryside, close to where the Nazi lines formed in World War II, Siroja was playing on a Finnish-built playground. It was donated by some business group that wanted to curry favor with the locals for a new joint venture. Children from the city always liked to stop by when they made family excursions to see the Czar's summer palace.

For some reason, as we watched Siroja zoom down the slides and swing on the swings, I mentioned President Nixon's name to Gulia.  I don't think I will ever recall exactly what we were discussing at the time. But Nixon's name seemed to start it all; the flood of confessions, the anonymous phone calls, the stories of treason and arms dealing, my visits to the most famous woman in the world, Jacqueline Bouvier Kennedy Onassis.  Soon she was sharing her suspicions of murder with me and her love for the dead spy, Gulia's best friend. But I couldn't remotely imagine that moment how far it would go.

It simply dropped out of the sky on me like a random raindrop from a single cloud that had survived, somehow, on an otherwise perfectly clear, sunny day. I almost wanted to laugh and ask, "Where on earth did that drop come from?"

Now I realize that first bit of the spy story was like a tiny drop of water in the Niagara River, just as it goes over the edge of the falls. All I knew that day was a brief outline of a tale of treason, like one wet speck in the river. But I felt the free-fall drop. Where that speck came from upstream was invisible. The mighty rush it belonged to was invisible. The breathtaking height of the falls was just a tug in my gut, and a rush of adrenaline keeping me alert. It was all just beginning, but I sensed I had gone over the edge all the same.

There was a hint of the same feeling 15 years later as I watched the mysterious waves from nowhere during my lunch at the Hotel du Cap-Eden-Roc in France. There was a hint of danger, yet nothing seemed to be threatened imminently.

The mystery deepened as Gulia told me about the little group that had organized to watch for signs of a Soviet nuclear attack on America. They had a network of people watching for the preparations. Before the attack there would be several telltale indications: the withdrawal of the Da Vinci's and some of the Rembrandt paintings from the Hermitage Museum; the disappearance of certain scientists and their families into secret bunkers; the protection of the diamond and gold collections in the Kremlin. At the other end, both French intelligence and Nixon were waiting for the news. They knew the coded signs, to be hidden in a cable about fencing match scores. The western plotters at the Paris fencing organization (*Fédération de l'Escrime Française*), would be watching.

Or alternately, if the ringleader could not send the fencing telex, any cable bearing or mentioning one man's name would be the sign for nuclear war. Gulia said that no one was an agent for the U.S. or organized by the West. They were self-starters, simply Russians who hated the prospect of their own country starting a nuclear war and thought Soviet Premier Nikita Khrushchev was truly dangerous. They initiated the links at a French-Russian fencing match in Leningrad. Nixon knew of the group and its credibility. No KGB disinformation was involved.

That was the story on the first day, anyway. I didn't yet know I was talking with the man whose name alone, if it appeared in a telex, would have announced World War III. Imagine being that man, living with the reality that your name was the trigger.

Why was he telling me this? That abiding mystery was to take 20 years to solve. But on that June day in 1991, under warm sunny skies outside Leningrad, I was simply baffled.

Gulia's best friend, Leonid, was the ringleader of the plot. Gulia explained that Leonid was arrested by the KGB in 1958 and imprisoned a mild three years because the KGB had only discovered some small details of the story, and not the purpose of the plot. Leonid had stashed survival supplies and radios in a cave in the Crimean Peninsula, his place to which he hoped he could flee if nuclear war was coming. But the discovery of radios and soap and basic supplies in the cave, by the Russian equivalent of Boy Scouts on a hike, did not give away that the people with the strange habits were national traitors.

In sight of the green walls of the Hermitage Museum that evening I asked Gulia just what response the group had expected from the West. Would not the warning have caused nuclear war? He seemed to be thrown off balance by the question. Was I accusing him of fomenting war? He gave a muddled response, but mostly indicated he hoped that a sharp warning from the West, and elimination of the surprise element, would have stopped the whole insanity.

That first day Gulia didn't quite admit that he personally had committed treason against the Soviet Union. But clearly, he had inside information and knew the traitors, led by Leonid, personally. He said (thus he must know, but how?) that the KGB had never learned of the little group's treason years ago. Even today its discovery could get people liquidated, he insisted. He told me their password among themselves (which I will not disclose).

What he didn't tell me that day was that the ringleader, Leonid, had just died a violent death in a car crash in France.

I had to assume Gulia was part of the group, and his revelation scared the hell out of me. It didn't say anything about this in the travel brochures. "See Russia and talk to traitors; hold their lives in your hands and share their secrets" was not a pitch I remembered.

As we headed back to town the sky darkened. By the time we reached the polling place where his wife was a monitor, a massive downpour was underway. Other little Ladas were completely disappearing around us into flooded potholes. With each footstep across the parking lot we risked disappearing into the deluge ourselves. It was almost as if a Soviet

God was trying to stop Yeltsin and the whole country from completing a legitimate election. Drowning seemed a very real possibility, literally and figuratively.

Working with Gulia, if that was going to be my future, was going to involve a lot of chaos and scrambling to keep my head above water. Were the gods angry with me and playing some cruel joke on me? Or were they presenting me with a huge opportunity to use my talents to bring order from chaos? Would I be swamped by this random wave, this revelation, this disruption, or would I sail on?

## Chapter 7

### *Après Le Déluge, Le Déluge*

After our perilous visit to the polling place, soaked but momentarily safe, Gulia dropped me off at his pal Boris's apartment where I was staying instead of in a hotel. In the old heart of Leningrad, in a crumbling Czarist era structure, Boris inhabited a building straight out of Dr. Zhivago. Built around a decrepit courtyard, the entry door, foyer and stairs looked like a construction site abandoned 70 years ago. I could imagine Communist revolutionary comrades making a point to destroy everything of bourgeois beauty.

His apartment consisted of two large rooms, each the size of a generous studio apartment. Probably it had been designed to hold two families, sharing the kitchen and bath (toilet in one room, tub and sink in another). The great hot water flow for a shower seemed to me like another staggering luxury, since such a rainfall showerhead is strictly illegal in parched Santa Barbara. But Boris had no idea his shower was a luxury.

Gulia said Boris inherited the apartment from his aunt. How could one person in

Russia have such lavish amounts of living space to himself? I wondered. What seemed like his good fortune when I arrived a few days earlier now seemed suspiciously excessive.

Unable to sleep, obsessed with the shock of the spy story, I made the notes in my journal by the light of my flashlight the size of a fat pen. I bought it for its compactness at Long's drugstore on State Street in Santa Barbara. I hate to stumble through the dark at night in a strange place. Suddenly my $3.59 travel accessory looked like the perfect spy's tool; something built to look like one thing that really is something different. Now it looked like something used to make secret notes of secret tales, which it was. Would it be introduced as evidence at my own spy trial? How would I explain that I just didn't want to stub my toe going to the bathroom, and anybody in Southern California can buy one? Certainly, nobody in Russia had one like it. Nobody in Russia had had a day like mine either.

Yeltsin had been elected President; I had been chosen to enter a secret world.

## Chapter 8

### *Nixon's The Good Guy And I Can't Sleep*

Nixon was a good guy in the story, cause enough for hesitation. Sleep was hopeless. The bizarre little Russian pillow, smelly from sour Russian soap, and my scratchy old blanket did not help lull me to sleep. Simply being in bed was a wildly foreign experience.

With the flashlight's thin beacon, I surveyed the Salvation-Army-1942-style furnishings of my bedroom as I made my notes. Gulia had arranged for me to stay with Boris, one of his old buddies near retirement age. Boris was peculiar, and Gulia explained it away saying Boris had gone through very bad times with the authorities. Was he a gulag survivor? Had he been tortured? (Yes!) He looked the part. His demeanor was subdued. His face and eyes abnormal. He looked like one of those zombies for whom the voodoo architects had worked. Yet he had been to Vegas! Vegas, for God's sake, was Boris's big memory of his trip to the US. What kind of gulag survivor on the outs with the authorities goes to Vegas? Was this apartment bugged? What kind of surveillance was I under? Just who the hell really were Gulia and Boris?

Debate replaced sleep; debate with myself whether I dared make notes of a spy plot unknown to the KGB. Very clearly Gulia had said that even now the KGB might liquidate people involved if they were exposed. They would probably just have accidents, not be arrested and tried.

Could I get out of the USSR with the notes? Was I insane to make them? Why would Gulia give me such power over his life, if I was right that he was involved? Was I insane to believe any of it? Who was this physicist telling me he committed treason? Why did he tell me? Maybe it was all hot air, calculated to impress me. Why did he help create the Soviet nuclear program and then undercut it? Why couldn't I let go of it and just let it be pleasant ramblings of a day in the country? Maybe he told me because he knew I wouldn't let go. But what did he want me to do with the story? Was I being recruited for something? Maybe he told me because I mentioned Nixon and he jumped to the conclusion that I was an agent or messenger. Maybe he had made a horrible mistake and realized it, so now my life was in danger. Maybe I had better get the first plane home. My mind raced along. After all, I had a three-year-old daughter

I had to determine if my life had been thrown into utter chaos, or if I'd been handed a golden opportunity. Gulia was clearly a man of incredible importance. And he had taken me into his confidence. But I couldn't tell if that was a good thing or a dangerous disaster. At least not yet.

I wanted my passport back from whomever Gulia had given it to. Passports of visiting foreigners had to be registered with the "militsia." If you stayed in a hotel it would be returned overnight. Mine had been gone several days for registration and I suddenly felt very vulnerable without it. I couldn't take the first plane home, or the second. Until I got that passport I was Boris's de facto prisoner. Could I skip out to the U.S. consulate? What would I say: "Hello, my name is Philip Myers and my host turns out to be a spy; could I please come in for a cup of coffee and a new passport?" How many hours, days, or weeks would it take to explain the predicament created in ten minutes of story-telling?

I hoped everything would be clearer in the morning. I was wrong. The next day we went to dinner at Professor Kolbyn's apartment to brainstorm (as I discovered five minutes beforehand) how to convert the entire Soviet military complex to peaceful uses, making use of six billion dollars' worth(!) of secret supplies of strategic metals in Leningrad warehouses.

Why the hell not!!??

The utter absurdity of me being handed a treasure trove of rare metals was very "...Woody Allen character stumbling through nuclear war." Jackie saw it immediately when I explained the events. But being so immersed in them, the humor was not as evident to me at first. Without the reservations that come from fear or the skepticism that comes from humor, I signed a contract with Professor Kolbyn's group giving me the right to look at various exotic technologies. And we talked about super-secret weapons programs involving biological computer chips that could be used to destroy the mind. What a charming way to deal with conquered populations or dissidents: just inject a biochip and control their brain!

I was a bit like a drunk who figured he was so far gone that one more sip won't matter. Of course, on the way I had to open my big mouth and tell Gulia that I thought the spy story would make a great movie. Suddenly I found myself (capitalist reflexes ruling) ignoring the weightiness of the matter and thinking about the next *Hard Copy* or *Movie of the Week*. And I wasn't even out of the country with my notes yet.

All this, of course, led to Jackie Kennedy telling me I'd end up squished in a trash can, but I get ahead of myself. She didn't enter the picture for six more months yet.

The trip had been such a whirlwind of meetings that I had gotten used to not knowing whom I was to meet until a few minutes before the session started. I had in mind doing a simple feasibility study about a computer programming venture. But Gulia constantly seemed to have bigger plans.

If I needed any further confirmation that I'd popped up on the radar of U.S. intelligence I got it in the duty-free shop at the airport as I left. As I was buying something another American went out of his way to chat with me. The assertive but polite middle-aged gentleman in a trench coat explained that he was assistant editor of a newspaper in Charleston, South Carolina. Charleston was home base to many American nuclear submarines, or "boomers," he informed me. His readers always liked to know what was happening with Russian boomers so he was in Leningrad to find out.

It wasn't exactly subtle. I had in my briefcase the authorization to offer Exxon six of the top-of-the-line Typhoon Soviet subs for conversion to Arctic drill rigs. OK, if our guys were watching me and wanted to know what I was up to I'd be an open book, I instantly decided. I told him I had a juicy scoop and would show him the authorization letter once we were on the plane. And I did. I'll forever believe that was a good decision and positively impacted U.S. intelligence's view of me. I was no rogue, amateur arms trader. I was just, well, what was I? I doubt they had a category for it. I was pretty sure my experience of the Soviet Union was far from run-of-the-mill.

# Chapter 9

## In Which A Lifeguard, And The Soviet Union, Go Glub Glub Glub

After that crazy week in Leningrad I decompressed at the Helsinki Intercontinental hotel for a day before starting the journey home.  It was a great reality check to have CNN again, croissants and a good sauna.  The Intercon's sauna is on the eighth floor, with a glass wall looking out onto the city.  In the searing heat and the western luxury, my past week in the Soviet Union took on a dreamlike quality.  I kept asking myself whether it had all really happened.  The next morning, I headed home, conveyed in first class courtesy of Pan Am frequent flyer miles. I was thrown back to the question of just who Gulia really was. After all, instead of a just launching a computer programming company, I was faced with figuring out how to deal with a story of treasonous conspirators, how to market a nuclear submarine fleet, and whether I could take over a super-secret biological computer chip technology (of course, only after the weapons application was mooted). Pretty much everything depended on Gulia at this early stage, and I had to be sure he wasn't trying to do a snow job on me.

I thought perhaps a little counsel was in order.

From Helsinki, I had phoned ahead to two pals who, I thought, could help me evaluate what had happened. I suggested we meet for lunch my first day back. Since I figured my own credibility was a possible issue in telling such a crazy tale about my first trip, I decided to skip any of the usual modest spots I frequent and pop in for lunch in the ever-so-establishment, ocean-view, patio restaurant at the five-star Four Seasons Santa Barbara Biltmore. During Reagan's years, the White House staff always stayed at the Biltmore when he was at his ranch. It was common to bump into Reagan's Attorney General, Ed Meese or White House Chief of Staff, James Baker, in the restaurant. In many ways it's the California version of the Hotel du Cap-Eden-Roc

I described my crazy experiences to Leo Fialkoff and Henry Huglin, two members of the Board of the Santa Barbara Committee on Foreign Relations who had been very kind to me. Leo was a "white" Russian, born in St. Petersburg/Leningrad about the time of the Communist revolution after which his family escaped to Finland.  During WWII, he was a U.S. Army liaison officer to the Red Army in Berlin. Later he had been given the job of preparing contingencies for the U.S. response to Stalin's death, when it was expected in the early 50's.  (Because of intra-Pentagon bickering about which military service had to give him office space, the project never got off the ground, and when Stalin died the U.S. had no array of contingency plans.)  Leo, I figured, should have a pretty good feel for Russian convolutions.  Leo said he would never return to St. Petersburg (he never called it Leningrad) until it was again called St. Petersburg.  Some years ago, Leo arranged for the British Foreign Office to invite me to spend a week at its country estate think tank, Wilton Park.

Henry was a retired Air Force General and senior NATO official. Once a syndicated columnist on foreign affairs, he was one of the very few members of the Santa Barbara Committee on Foreign Relations who separately held membership in the Council on Foreign Relations in New York.

Henry and Leo didn't think I was crazy. That was good. But as for really getting a handle on what was going on, that was another matter. After all, there wasn't much precedent for ways of dealing with an "open" Soviet Union. Thanks to Gorbachev's

"Glasnost" and "Perestroika," all the rules were in doubt. All kinds of things that had been unthinkable, or laden with meaning in the past, had become routine.

Despite the "anything's possible" atmosphere, I decided that after my through-the-looking-glass first trip, I had to determine if I wanted to ever set foot in the Soviet Union again.  Much of the issue boiled down to Gulia's credibility.  So, I set out to see if I could check out Gulia's story of espionage.

If his story of treason and advanced warning of nuclear war were published and widely known, I reasoned, then he was full of hot air. His insistence that it was unknown would be exposed as mere hype, probably designed to impress me by looking important and "friendly" to Americans. Sorting out who's real and who's hype in overseas business is often eighty percent of the problem. If Gulia was engaging in blatant self-puffery, then I would forget about the whole Russian thing.  A second trip would require real money instead of frequent flyer miles on a dying airline.  I wasn't about to waste time or money if my confidence level in the people I had to deal with wasn't high.

If nothing about Gulia's spy story had been published, it would only mean the story might be true, and his credibility maybe was intact, and his insider importance might be as-presented. I figured there was no way to obtain real confirmation, unless I could get Richard Nixon to talk.

So, I did two things. First, I decided to do a very quiet literature and data base search to see if anything had been published about the spy conspiracy. Secondly, I wrote to Nixon.

Nixon's White House Chief of Staff, Bob Haldeman, coincidentally had moved to Santa Barbara and joined the Committee on Foreign Relations. Thus, I knew him a bit from there and a couple other groups in town. But I didn't want to involve him at this early research stage. The connection to Haldeman was too slight.

There is extensive literature about other American spy stories of the Cold War, especially about CIA moles in the KGB or Russian military intelligence (GRU) named Popov and Penkovsky. If a story as dramatic as Gulia's were true and had been published anywhere, it should be easy to find, I figured.

But I didn't want to draw attention to myself by doing the searching, especially in data bases accessible from my desktop computer. At that point I had to assume, because of telexes that had been going to the Soviet Union about submarines, that any computer searches might be watched by the NSA and/or the Soviets. And I wanted to stay under the radar with this odd subject of treason. Instead I hired what I thought would be the least notable researcher who could do everything without attracting attention.

Setting out on this crazy quest to check out my bolt-out-of-the-blue spy story ended up really setting the course of my next twenty-five years, for better or worse.

Joe Hickman, the lifeguard at the pool where I swam daily, was a UCSB history major, and the perfect person to do some snooping. I briefed Joe on as much of the story as I thought he needed to know, and carefully instructed him to discuss it with no one. All I wanted was to know what he could find in openly available sources.

Completely in contradiction, however, to my desire to be low key, I also decided to write directly to Richard Nixon. Finding his office address in New Jersey proved not to be too difficult. Since the phone wasn't listed, I called Republican Central Committee headquarters in the suburban New Jersey County where I thought he lived. They did not know the address, but someone in the office remembered the name of a travel agency in the same building as his office. I tracked down the travel agency, and of course, they knew that they were sharing an edifice with the former President. So, I couldn't phone but I could write.

In a mailgram (basically an email printed out and delivered with the mail in those day) I explained a little about the story I had been told in Russia and asked if he could comment upon its veracity. I added that he could easily check me out as many local Republican notables like Holmes Tuttle and Brooks Firestone in Santa Barbara knew me from my 1980 run for the California State Assembly.

Nixon never wrote back. Instead, total confirmation of the story was given to Lifeguard Joe in the oddest of ways, both scaring him to death and tipping me off that my phone and/or office were bugged.

After a weekend at home in California's Central Valley, Joe came into my office and told me about his own "through-the-looking glass" experience. It had taken him two days to work up the courage to tell me, for fear that I would think he had violated the rules and blabbed something that precipitated a discussion about the story. He did not know I had written to Nixon.

The night he got the confirmation started innocently enough. While home in Porterville, California for the weekend, his high school buddy "Lara" invited him over for dinner. When he arrived, he discovered that her Uncle Curt was visiting for the first time in several years. Uncle Curt Struble, it turned out, was a Foreign Service officer who had been posted at the U.S. Consulate in Leningrad.

Uncle Curt proceeded, over dinner, to tell Gulia's story in enough detail as to make it unmistakable. He explained that he had learned it from a professor at Berkeley, Martin Malia.

Malia, I discovered with a little checking, had been a Nixon advisor on Russia and also appeared to have a classic intelligence background, with language training at the military's Monterey School of Languages and service in the Navy. You don't have to be a rocket scientist to figure that young Navy officers in the 1950's who were sent to special Russian language school probably did more than serve drinks at Embassy parties. Malia more recently had generated great controversy when he wrote an article under the pseudonym "Z", arguing, while Gorbachev was still in power and popular in the West, that Gorbachev would bring neither democracy nor a market economy to Russia.

So, unless you believe in billion-to-one coincidences, the researcher to whom I had given the job of looking for confirmation of Gulia's story had been handed that confirmation, after I wrote to Nixon, by a source traceable to Nixon. My oh my. It seemed like it would have been a lot easier for Nixon just to send a postcard, but that's before I entered the world of "plausible deniability," i.e., a typical intelligence community trick to make the arrangement of an entanglement or event completely deniable. For whatever reason, and I certainly had to wonder about it, I had been given my confirmation, and I had also been kept at arms-length, with Nixon as the source of the confirmation being plausibly deniable.

As Joe told his story, expecting my disbelief and a reproach, he was surprised to have me pull him out of the office for a walk around the block. Nobody else, not even my wife, knew about Joe and his research project. Nobody knew, that is, unless the phone and/or office were bugged.

As we strolled through the nearby city gardens I enlightened Joe as to the Nixon contact and the apparent bugging. I kept wondering what on earth I had gotten into. I was stunned that Nixon would go to the trouble to provide confirmation but not want it to be straightforward. But why had Nixon bothered to give me the confirmation at all? I was as baffled as when I asked myself why Gulia told me the story in the first place.

Joe drove back home and got his gun. For at least the next year I'm afraid he assumed every van parked in front of his apartment was filled with CIA or KGB agents waiting to liquidate him. My God, it was fun to work with Joe.

Whatever was going on, clearly Gulia was legitimate and somebody wanted me to know it. So I started planning my second trip. My venture capitalist friends who saw my research report from the first trip suggested other issues about software development that needed work. I would go back to figure out more of the specifics of computer programming. And I would see if Gulia would offer more about the story.

August 1991, I was scheduled to go for the second trip. The Typhoon submarine project had quieted down and it looked like I would really be able to focus on computer programming. Early in the month, however, Gulia started to offer uncharacteristic resistance. Suddenly he was saying that everyone I should meet with would be away on vacation. Baffled, I sent a list of the most critical names and asked specifically if they would be out of town. The others did not matter much to me.

There was no answer, just again a suggestion that I should delay the trip. So, I went to San Francisco. And the Soviet Union had an attempted coup d'état.

My wife tiptoed into the guest bedroom in a friend's house on Nob Hill in San Francisco to wake me up and deliver the bad news. As soon as I picked up my heart off the floor, I jumped out of bed and turned on CNN. Oh God, my Russian adventure looked like a total write-off. There were Gorbachev's hard-liners he'd appointed to the Cabinet claiming that they were in charge now. I felt sick. I wondered about Gulia. Was he being melted down for the gold in his teeth? Later he confessed that the KGB chief, Kruchkov, who participated in the attempted coup, or putsch, had given a speech before the putsch that singled him out as an enemy of the State. Kruchkov had railed against Russians who worked too closely with foreigners, and especially those who worked too closely with liberal western universities, and especially those who collaborated with the Stanford Center for International Security and Arms Control (CISAC). There was only one CISAC alum in Leningrad: Gulia.

And yet, intuition told me that Gulia somehow had known about the putsch in advance. His urgings that I delay the trip and his inadequate explanations suggested he was clued in. If so, he probably had taken some measure to protect himself, if he had to protect himself.

Over the next couple days Russian Republic President Yeltsin, a former ally of Gorbachev, stood on a tank and denounced the putsch, and then spoke on an open phone line from the Russian White House (the legislative home, akin to the U.S. Capitol) with President Bush. Little-known was the fact that the phone line used a satellite link and phone from the nearby American business center in the Moscow Radisson Hotel. As historical oddity would have it, a partner in the business center was none other than Nixon's White House Chief of Staff, Bob Haldeman. Haldeman, a Santa Barbaran, later told me the story of his partner running over to the Russian White House during the coup with the satellite phone so as to circumvent any effort of the KGB to cut off phone links. Haldeman's partner was later mysteriously assassinated in Moscow, perhaps as revenge for his role in stopping the putsch.

Because of Yeltsin's firm resistance, the putsch collapsed into comic opera in short form. I saw a news report that bulldozers placed on the airport runway near Gorbachev's vacation home to block his movements had been removed, and he was flying back to Moscow. Elated I telexed to Gulia that since the runways were clear and everyone was now heading home from vacation, perhaps we should look immediately at rescheduling my trip. Within twenty-four hours he gave the unequivocal response that everything was now OK and I should get myself to Leningrad as quickly as possible. Two weeks after the coup attempt, much to my mother's distress, I was in Russia again.

With new confidence that Gulia was an extraordinary character, tied into extraordinary sources of information, I decided to bet the farm on my relationship with him. The entrepreneur in me said that something really grand was possible from knowing him.

## Chapter 10

### *Computer Programming Is Fun*

Finding the right plausible business venture with Gulia took a lot of effort. Computer programming seemed pretty interesting thanks to the suggestion of my venture capital pal, Keith Geeslin. Programming is what Igor did.

On my first trip to Leningrad in 1991, bearing my submarine drill-rig technical paper, Gulia had introduced me to Igor, a wiry middle-aged professor. He was head of a small quasi-private company offering computer programming services to foreign companies. And he was a highly-accomplished professor of Applied Mathematics at the Politechnic University, more or less their version of Cal-Tech or M.I.T. His little group already had its first foreign contract. Gulia thought they might make the perfect nucleus of a software outsourcing venture. And my primary mission, notwithstanding nuclear submarines, was to do a feasibility study of a programming company. To me it seemed much easier and more reasonable than submarine conversion projects.

Igor used to read banned books under a blanket in bed using a flashlight, and not very long before I met him in Leningrad. His daughter told me about the books over dinner. And clearly his mother, also at dinner, had not approved. She was very old-school and appreciated how the Soviets had allowed her to escape her village and get an engineering education in Moscow. I thought of my own engineer wife who suggested the submarine drill-rig adaptation and her stories of fighting sexism in the field.

Still, Gulia wanted to show me around and have me take a look at lots of different projects. And Igor wanted to take me to a sports resort to swim and play tennis. As it happens, we made time for both.

Other than computer programming, Gulia's top priority was the submarine drillship idea. Rubine (Ruby in Russian), was the "design bureau" for the Typhoon Nuclear Submarine Fleet. Americans had never gone there before. The day before we went, Gulia told me that the head of Rubine was also head of the equivalent of the U.S. Armed Services Committee in the Russian Duma (parliament). Mr. Spassky was intensely interested in the idea of converting the submarines his group had designed into oil drill rigs, or at least of adapting the technology to produce a new design of underwater rigs. Plus, said Gulia, it would allow them to build bigger and better submarine tankers to deliver the oil. They already had them, he noted: tankers of 100,000 tons, utter monster submarines.

So, of course, I thought I would mention the tanker advantage to Mr. Spassky. Alas, it seems that the existence of submarine tankers was classified and I was not supposed to know Mr. Spassky had built them. He seemed rather taken back.

Since I was not arrested or dragged off to Siberia for knowing classified Soviet information, I merely plowed ahead with our discussion. Churchill may have thought Russia was a "riddle wrapped in a mystery inside an enigma," but for my purposes it was just plain daffy. Or maybe the whole damn country had been scripted by Woody Allen.

The more bizarre things got in Russia the more I wanted to just tell everyone to quit trying so hard to be complex. But you don't undo 70 years of distorted motivations overnight. It takes quite a bit of reading under blankets by flashlight I concluded.

Apparently, I had not offended Mr. Spassky, as he proposed that I approach Exxon and Chevron about buying a few monster Typhoon submarines. Bold as I am, I still thought that it was unlikely Exxon and Chevron would take me seriously if I merely phoned up and told them I'd like to sell them a few nuclear subs for conversion to drillships.

The whole notion went past Woody Allen towards Dr. Strangelove. Or at least I thought it would look that way to the big oil companies. Perhaps I was training the Russians too well and too quickly to not let anything stand in their way. As the Nike ads say, "Just do it." Woody Allen might do it, but at least it struck me as not a very good idea to call Exxon out of the blue with an offer of nuclear subs.

Thus, obligingly Mr. Spassky arranged for a letter of authorization that I drafted to be signed at the Defense Ministry and couriered to me from Moscow overnight. There being no FedEx or equivalent, I knew that it was a big deal for someone to show up from Moscow at my doorstep the next morning at 6:30 a.m. with the signed document that was only discussed the day before in Leningrad.

Oh, great, I was in the nuclear sub business now! And all because my wife opened her mouth over cookies and tea. Frankly, I really didn't want to buy or broker the sale of six nuclear submarines. I wanted to do computer programming.

Focus Focus Focus!!! Swim Swim Swim!!! Stay grounded.

Igor's offer to have a sports day was just what I needed.  He rounded up a medical student, Oleg, who was dating his daughter, and off we went to the Club Med equivalent beach resort that belonged to some factory.  It was a somewhat seedy version of a Holiday Inn with two tennis courts, a gym, and an indoor pool. By Soviet standards, however, it was pretty luxurious.  And I definitely appreciated the pool.  I also appreciated beating Oleg at tennis despite his being 15 years younger.

Oleg was great for enlightening me on the oddities of economic life in the Soviet Union.  First of all, at the medical school he pointed out that the word for "corpse" in Russia is "troop." Had anyone in Russia thought that joining the army was, perhaps, not a great future for them?  Then again it wasn't a volunteer army.

We talked about the shortages of everything and the informal (black market) channels for acquiring medicines and medical supplies.  I was stunned that Band-Aids did not exist. And Russian condoms were considered worthless and totally unreliable. I thought I could get doctors in Santa Barbara to donate supplies of free sample drugs they get all the time from drug companies. It was a big happy surprise when I also got large donations of condoms!

Oleg said he would be able to make lots of money if I could bring him any such things. His state scholarship was a ridiculously small amount, and his dorm was a slum. He picked up extra money giving "Tashkent" style vigorous massages to tourists and expats. But condoms and medical supplies would be HUGE. So, I promised to see if I could bring some back on my next trip.

This led to the absurd moment at Russian customs of the agent asking me if the bag with over 500 condoms was for my personal use. When I assured him it was, I imagine he could figure out that most Americans are not that oversexed. But he let me pass, and I think I made a dorm full of Russian medical students very, very happy.

But bit by bit, between anecdotes of banned books read under the blankets, and submarine tankers that don't exist but do, and crazy condom supply lines, I was catching on to how the Soviet Union worked. It was more Rube Goldberg than Woody Allen, but close enough. Jackie's instincts were proving to be totally correct.

## Chapter 11

### *Kaboom: Now I'm A Counter-Terrorist*

The second major project that was to occupy me for many years started quite accidentally, after my second trip to the USSR. I became a counter-terrorist.

Chris Silva was the son of one of my legal clients, a sweet little old lady declining fast due to Alzheimer's Disease. Chris would come to Santa Barbara from time to time to check up on her and to have lunch with me to see if any legal fine-tuning of her documents was required. As we finished our review he asked me what else I'd been up to lately. He got a quick overview of two trips to the Soviet Union and Gulia's influential role in putting defense technologies into business ventures.

Chris looked at me oddly and asked, "Do you know what I do?"

"Nope, not a clue." All I knew was that he lived in D.C.

"I'm in counter-terrorism for the FAA. It's my job to find explosives detection technology anywhere in the world. We've heard rumors that the Russians have something but we haven't been able to get anywhere near it. Do you think you can?" he asked.

Chris went on to explain that they'd had an offer from someone that for $100,000 they could be put in touch with a classified bomb detection program via a maze of in-laws and acquaintances. "We don't do that," he explained.

Well, Gulia was certainly the right guy to ask. So I did. A couple weeks later I was back in Russia at Boris's apartment. And thanks to Gulia three KGB colonels in uniform arrived with briefcases stuffed with documents about a bomb detection machine for carry-on luggage. A prototype was almost ready for deployment at the local airport. The technology had just been declassified and spun out of a government lab into a private company (still with some government ownership).

From the stacks of documents covering the coffee table we selected about ten pages that summarized the machine's design and capabilities.

"We need beezness partner. You be our beezness partner, please! You friend of Dr. Gulia," the KGB boys said with enthusiasm.

It cost me exactly zero, not $100,000. I drafted on the spot a handwritten contract on blue KLM in-flight stationary giving me worldwide rights outside of Russia to the technology. I had no idea what I'd gotten myself into. My entire knowledge of explosives detection and counter-terrorism came from ten minutes with Chris Silva and an hour with the KGB guys. It was one hell of a fast tutorial. But my gut feel was that those documents indicated that the Russians had something very valuable.

I flew home and faxed the documents to Chris. Within minutes he was on the phone almost breathless asking how the hell I'd ever gotten the documents out of Russia. And he insisted I catch the red-eye to D.C. to meet his boss, Dr. Lyle Malotky, head of security technology for the FAA. (Later, after the 9/11 attacks on the World Trade Center, Malotky held the same position with the Department of Homeland Security.) That first day the lanky, brainy Malotky was very clear about one thing: I needed a US partner to help submit a proposal for support and cooperation to the FAA. The partner would have to have the necessary security clearance to know the minimum number of grams of explosives the FAA wanted to be able to detect. (eventually I learned it was 250 grams, as 300 grams, i.e. about 2/3 of a pound, was enough to blow a hole the in the side of a plane and bring it down). Malotky suggested I talk to SWL (previously known as Special Weapons Lab), which conveniently had a branch in Santa Barbara.

Thus, began a long saga of trying to build FAA cooperation, and later a proposal to the Office of Naval Intelligence, extensive discussions with the CIA's In-Q-Tel venture fund for security technologies, and millions in funding ultimately from NATO for a key Russian lab. That story of trying to get western money to pay for technology development in sensitive Russian labs is a book in itself.

But because of my initial success in finding what Chris Silva asked for he called back a few months later. He had a new favor to ask. The FAA had heard rumbles that the Soviets had a new kind of explosive, dramatically more powerful than C-4 or Semtex, the usual plastic explosives of choice of suicide bombers and airplane terrorists. The concern was that only a tiny amount would be needed to bring down a plane. And that amount would be too small to be detected by any technology on the horizon.

As it happened, I was due to call Gulia in ten minutes so I added the question to our agenda. To my amazement, he said immediately that he knew the professor who had developed the "hypervelocity explosives" and he volunteered to give him a call when we hung up. Twenty minutes later he called back confirming that yes, hypervelocity explosives existed and were ten times more powerful than C-4. But the inventor thought it was no threat to planes. It had been developed for mining and detonation required a stick of dynamite. Thus, the dynamite was easily detectable if anyone tried to get it onto a plane. Gulia said the professor was happy to set up some joint testing with the FAA and they should call him to arrange a meeting.

Feeling exceedingly efficient I called Chris back with his answer within 30 minutes of getting the question. There was something like a gurgling, stunned mumble on his end and he announced he'd have to get back to me. OK, I had plenty to keep me busy in the meantime. After a week, I wondered why I hadn't heard from him. After a month, I was annoyed. After six months, he finally called back. Frankly I'd pretty much forgotten about the hypervelocity explosives.

"We want to come debrief you in person," he announced when he finally called back. He proposed bringing someone from the Defense Intelligence Agency (DIA) with him.

"But Chris, I already told you everything I know. For a good time, call Gulia; he'll set up everything. It's a waste of time to come see me," I urged.

No, he insisted they had to see me. So, a couple of weeks later I had Chris and the DIA fellow sitting in my office in Santa Barbara asking me to repeat everything. It was ridiculous. "Just call Gulia," I told them.

"Oh no, we could never get clearance to talk directly to a Russian," the DIA man replied. "It took us six months to get clearance to come talk to you!"

Unbelievable! I was exasperated, bemused, stunned and surely said a few offensive things. Trying to salvage the situation the DIA guy then proposed that next time I went to Russia I just get a chunk of the explosives and bring it back in my suitcase. I thought it was the dumbest thing anyone had ever said to me. He was proposing that I carry an unknown explosive through at least three airports with no official authorization or role or any kind and no precise idea of the characteristics of the stuff. Insanity!

Our meeting quickly ended. And I decided to add to the Typhoon Security Technology business plan a project to test and understand hypervelocity explosives and determine how they could be detected.  If the US government couldn't get it together to do the job, I could.

While a plane might not be at risk from the hypervelocity explosives, thought I, a seaport surely was from a ship loaded up with the stuff. No one would be able to scan a ship for a stick of dynamite!  With some radioactive elements added it could become a fearsome dirty bomb.  When I mentioned it later to the head of counter-terrorism for the Netherlands regarding security for the Port of Rotterdam, he was extremely alarmed. So, I felt my instincts were on target. It is a classic example of bureaucratic short-sightedness that the FAA was only concerned about the threat to planes, and absolutely nothing was done despite the obvious threat in any situation where  stick of dynamite would go undetected, as on a ship or even in a suicide bomber's vest.  The FAA only looked at threats to aviation. But my private company, Typhoon Security Technology, was staring at a huge commercial opportunity.

At least Chris and the DIA had pointed me at a new opportunity in counter-terrorism. If our own government was too dense to pick up the ball and run with it, I would do so within the context of Typhoon Security Technology Inc.

# Chapter 12

## *Jackie Signs On*

New Year's Eve day 1991 was slow around the office. Everyone else had gone home early. I stayed on for a bit of rare contemplation, trying to figure out how to make 1992 top 1991. It was a tall order, since 1991 had been a whirlwind year, with my first two business trips to Russia bracketing the coup that destroyed the Soviet Union. Having had Gulia take me into his confidence about the Cold War spy plot, I was left with the difficult issue of what to do with the story.

Early on I had set up a meeting in Hollywood with a video distributor I knew and his pal, former head of talent at ABC who later became Pierce Brosnan's agent. While there was interest in the story they wanted to update it to be about me stumbling my way into a den of spies. GOOD GOD NO! My business efforts and the spy tale had to be kept separate, completely compartmentalized. It couldn't help me do business in Russia or with the explosives detection people from the KGB if I were portrayed on the big screen cavorting with traitors.  At that moment, I thought I could keep those tracks from crossing. Why I was so naïve as to think so is something I still wonder about. It seems a tad ludicrous in retrospect.  But I thought I could do so by ditching the movie idea and going a different direction rather than abandoning it altogether.

With my feet on the desk, as the last hours of 1991 ticked away, I thought that perhaps it would be better to start off telling Gulia's story with a book project rather than a movie. Knowing not a soul in the book world, I was stumped on where to start. But then I recalled that Leonid had collaborated on a book with Jackie Kennedy. I had initially dismissed going to her, assuming that she would not touch something as hot as a true spy story, especially where she knew the number one spy.  It seemed to be too full of possibilities for wild tabloid stories for me to believe she would be interested in being involved. But finally, I figured I had nothing to lose. Why not let her make that judgment call? And if she said no, at least I could show Gulia that I'd made a serious effort to go to the top.

With some recollection of news stories that she worked at Doubleday Publishing, I first called George Doubleday in San Francisco, a friend and a distant relative of the publishing Doubledays.  He explained that the company had been sold years ago to a German conglomerate (Bertelsman) and he no longer had any contacts there. Although he knew Ted and Joan Kennedy as a young man who frequented Cape Cod, he couldn't help me with any introductions to Jackie. It was all too remote.

Lacking any obvious proper introduction, I simply called New York directory assistance and got Doubleday Publishing's number. I asked the switchboard for Mrs. Onassis' secretary and, in a flash, I was talking to her assistant, Scott Moyers. I didn't think it was supposed to be this easy!

She was gone for the holidays, but Scott seemed intrigued by a short description of the story. He asked me to fax him a few paragraphs summarizing the story and how I bumped into it so he could show Mrs. Onassis. Realistically I figured I'd get a polite "drop dead" note and hear nothing more about it. But at least I'd have something to show Gulia that I had tried.

The next day it occurred to me that she might wonder, beyond the quick summary of how I happened to be in Russia, just who I was. To address her potential curiosity, or allow her to check me out, I faxed my resume to Scott as well figuring it might increase the chances she really would look at the project. On paper I looked like a pretty solid citizen, a Phi Beta Kappa graduate of Stanford and member of enough community Boards of Directors to clearly differentiate me from the average couch potato. Especially useful, perhaps, for her was my association with the Council on Foreign Relations. Her longtime companion, Maurice Templesman, was a member of the Council. I figured I ought to give her some easy way to determine whether or not I was legitimate.

Nonetheless, I was completely shocked when right after New Year's I checked my answering machine to hear:

***"Ah, Mr. Myers. It's Jacqueline Onassis in New York on Wednesday morning January 8th at 11:10. If you could call me at 212 492 9747. The mornings are best for me. But, uh, I'm fascinated by your, what you sent me and I'd love to talk about it."*** (Listen to it at Facebook.com/PhilMyersAuthor)

The voice was unmistakable. As soon as I came down off the ceiling, I returned the call. Expecting a woman aloof, unapproachable and idiosyncratic, I was floored to find her open, candid and very funny. During 20 minutes I described how I had come across the story. At first, she reacted to my experience saying it was just one of the wonderful things that happen out of the blue.

Jackie recounted how she had worked closely with Leonid on the book that former *VOGUE* magazine editor Diana Vreeland who had become curator of costumes at the Metropolitan Museum of Art had asked her to do. One of her first books was "In the Russian Style." And she seemed especially intrigued when I told her that Gulia told me about Leonid's presumed romance with a young French fencer at the time the spy plot was hatched during a Franco-Russian fencing match in Leningrad in 1956.

As I elaborated upon the story she found it all very convoluted and startled me saying,

**"You're going to end up squished in a trash can somewhere."**

I stared at the phone in astonishment, bemused but also alarmed. I could not fathom her tossing off quotes like that. Somehow having Jacqueline Kennedy Onassis, the lady in the pink suit, scrambling on the back of the limousine to pick up pieces of JFK's skull, of all people, tell me she thought I could get squished, seemed to give it reality. I really didn't know what to make of her reaction, but it was a jolt nonetheless.

As I talked on in that first call, about the tale of how I had heard the story, she compared me to a Woody Allen character stumbling around in a nuclear war film. And she was hooked. She said she had sent my fax to Karl Katz, a curator at the Metropolitan Museum of Art who introduced her to Leonid. Because he did film and TV work, she wanted his thoughts on handling the story, perhaps as a documentary. She also thought that Karl had tried to help Leonid, for whom money in the States was an ongoing issue. Mrs. Onassis described the inside of Leonid's apartment on 96th St. in Manhattan, only a few blocks from her own. She thought it was quite modest, giving an example of a simple table covered by a scarf or cloth.

Jackie also described how the book they worked on together, *In the Russian Style*, had been subjected to a nasty review in *The New York Review of Books* by Nicholas Nabokov, who disparaged her editorial talents. Jackie explained that Leonid had leapt to her defense with a series of letters to the editor, Bob Silvers, defending the points attacked by Nabokov and responding to Nabokov's self-defense. She spoke of Leonid with great warmth and appreciated clearly his championing of her professional reputation against Nabokov's very personal and condescending criticism.

Jackie also claimed she was trying to get in to see Stephen Rubin, publisher of

Doubleday, about the story. She laughed and said she'd try to corner him coming out of the restroom and try to talk about it. She thought that maybe they could get a writer in the genre to do the project. (Tom Clancy, I thought..?!) I had a hard time envisioning Jackie lurking in the hallway to catch her boss coming out of the john. But I thought it was an utterly charming way of downplaying her ability to get his attention.

Jackie also thought she might want to talk about the story with her friend, Jann Wenner, publisher of *Rolling Stone*, and with movie producer Mark Nichols, an old beau and now married to ABC superstar Diane Sawyer (she had presided at the 1990 meeting of the Council on Foreign Relations where my adventure began). Talk about picking up the ball and running with it. I kicked myself for not having gone to her sooner.

We agreed to talk again soon, after she had some more reaction from a few people. I told her that Gulia was likely to be in New York in the near future, and she thought it might be interesting to meet him and hear firsthand about Leonid's exploits.

That day I sent a telex to Gulia informing him that I had spoken to "the famous woman in New York who knew your old fencing friend.

She is extremely interested in the book possibilities and we would likely meet with her when you are here."

Gulia sent back a shocking response which even now I do not understand: "Be careful with famous women.  Don't let them cheat you.  You are so kind and trustful." Maybe I had played my "Innocent Abroad" image too strongly.  If anyone in the whole world was not likely to cheat me, with all the messiness that such double-dealing entails, it was Jackie. Gulia's response baffled me. Even more baffling was his quick reversal. And I was totally confused by Jackie's response to the situation. I was still astonished that she had not only taken an interest in the story but had grabbed on tight. Sorting out and making sense of everyone's motivations was not to be a quick process.

Two days after the first conversation I spoke again with her. She said that Karl Katz had been "overcome" by the information, and that his first reaction was that Leonid's death must not have been an accident.

"Not an accident" I thought!!!  What the hell is going on here?  The man who introduced Jackie to Leonid has just told her Leonid must have been murdered. What did he know that I didn't? And furthermore, here was

Jackie passing along murder suspicions to me. For someone who was supposed to crave privacy and stand above the fray, it seemed like a pretty dicey thing to pass along to me, a comparative stranger. What nerve had I struck? Getting squished in a trash can seemed again a little more real. This was just getting too bizarre.

She said she asked Karl if he had had a clue about Leonid's past, and that he claimed he did not. But in retrospect, a few remarks Leonid had made that he recalled now made sense. She also said Leonid had left two children and that Karl had tried to set up a trust fund for their education. Jackie said she had donated to it (probably she was the $20,000 anonymous donor I later learned about). Jackie said she had asked Karl Katz to call me.

Jackie also said that Doubleday publisher Rubin had not been too keen on the story, feeling that there was a surplus of Russian book projects around because of the recent collapse of the Soviet Union. His suggestion was to go to Hollywood first and get it done there, then do a book. I held my breath, wondering if my book with Jackie had just dead-ended. Not at all!

If Rubin didn't want it for Doubleday, she would proceed on her own with me and bring in someone to help. She said she thought it would not work in a fictionalized version, and that it should be done as non-fiction with a superb writer. She would try to do some legwork for me and look around for a good writer and show the idea to some screenwriters.

I was incredulous that Jackie was picking up the story, with a new murder angle, and running with it full speed even though Doubleday's publisher, her boss, had passed on it. Her confidence in the story (or her curiosity about Leonid's past) inspired me to stick with it. At least then and there that's what I thought. Years later the possibility arose that she may have been a CIA agent working with Leonid and she needed to know what I knew about his death and their work. But that possibility, which I discuss later, hadn't arisen yet. At the moment it seemed to be the merits of the story and her personal curiosity about the death of her friend that was the source of her interest.

Right then and there I figured I would let Jackie "make the call" as to how to structure the project. Whatever illustrious help she wanted to bring in was perfectly OK with me. After all, the book project remained an afterthought, a sideline to my real business of computer programming. And I thought she was the expert in publishing to whom I should listen.

Four days later we spoke again for an update. She said she thought she might show it to Mort Janklow, one of the biggest literary agents in New York. Janklow, she explained, had been Senator Moynihan's lawyer but had shifted to books and movies and partnered with a woman, Lynn Nesbitt. Jackie wasn't very keen on me getting stuck having to pay a high-priced agent like Janklow. But she wanted to show it to him anyway. She also thought it unlikely I'd find a good publisher unless I first hired a good writer, for $50-$60,000. She cautioned me that "you'll be taken for a ride unless you know this world."

Jackie surprised me by announcing she'd asked the *New York Review of Books* to send her copies of the exchange of letters between Leonid and Nabokov over Nabokov's criticism of her 1976 book *In the Russian Style*. She wanted me to see it. A short time later it arrived with a nice note from her saying, "Here is the correspondence I told you about. It isn't as long as I remembered and perhaps only of marginal interest, but you will enjoy reading it."

She asked me if she could send a letter about the story to the *New York Review of Books* editor Bob Silvers to get his opinion. She doubted the *New York Review of Books* would be the way to go. "They're so ivory tower they can get on your nerves," explained Jackie. But she also clearly valued Silver's input to her thinking about how the story should be handled. Of course, I agreed to let her do as she thought best. I felt that anything Jackie wanted to do for me I could easily accept.

I later had a conversation with Mr. Silvers in which he showed great interesting in the story, envisioning an article written by Gulia about it as the cover story in *New York Review of Books.* I'm sure I never would have gotten his attention but for Jackie opening the door which she had done without hesitation. Her kindness in protecting me and mentoring me through a process and an industry I didn't know at all was really touching. The lawyer in me, of course, knew that the textbook thing to do was to have her sign a confidentiality agreement, and ask that anyone to whom she showed the story do the same. But it was pretty inconceivable to me that she would steal a story, and just as inconceivable that anyone in her circle would cross her by doing so.

I promised to send her a translation of a Russian interview with Leonid I had found. She seemed very thirsty for any information about Leonid I could offer. She exclaimed, "I just want to really help Leonid." She explained that Karl indicated that Leonid had told him in little bits how hard life has been in the Soviet Union.  Leonid had lost his job at the Hermitage Museum and spent three years in a Siberian prison camp.  After that he never was able to regain a prestigious position in Russia and worked for a while as a janitor at the museum. Only when he got to New York was he able to regain a curator's lofty position, at the Metropolitan Museum of Art.

She said Karl had been very emotional about it all, and our discussion edged again into questions of physical danger to me and a possible murder of Leonid.  I downplayed it, and she answered, "If you're American you don't live in that paranoid way." Her tone had a cautionary bent to it, as if perhaps I'd be well advised to ratchet up my paranoia a little bit. I did.

She ended the call saying, "I feel privileged that you got in touch with me.  You sound really nice on the phone."  From the bottom of my heart I responded that I thought she was very kind and I appreciated her help. In retrospect, it seems quite remarkable that she never once had a conversation about any compensation for herself from the project. Her only interest was in "helping Leonid" as she put it, which I took to mean providing some revenue to his children and burnishing Leonid's reputation.

Since Karl Katz had not contacted me, I decided to track him down myself. I called the Metropolitan Museum but was told he recently had gone off to another position. But they offered to pass along a message to him. A few minutes later he called me. He said he was "stunned" by the enormity of what Leonid had done. He chatted a bit about his old friend Leonid and indicated that he was very fond of the man and used to greet him effusively when they used the same entrance to the museum. He explained that Leonid's children were "fairly needy" and volunteered that he would try to find their addresses for me. He also recounted how excited Leonid had been the first time he met Jackie, even to the point of polishing the buttons on his blazer.

But when I told him Jackie had mentioned his comments that Leonid must have been murdered, he back-pedaled fast and ended the conversation. From his tone, I was sure he was surprised that Jackie had repeated the murder suspicions to me. And Karl never called me back with the children's addresses. I found them with Gulia's help. As the mysteries deepened, and the Metropolitan Museum was revealed as a hotbed of intelligence agency types as I'll explain, I decided to stay away, not sure just what was going on there.

I briefed Gulia again on my conversations with Jackie, and back came a new telex saying: "Encouraged by your talk with genious (sic) lady. God bless her and her initiatives." OK, I had a green light to proceed, for Gulia was pleased. But I confess I remained baffled just why he would want the story to come out. Gulia would often say that his primary motivation was to assure that Leonid not be a forgotten soldier of the Cold War. But as I was later to sort out, the investigation of Leonid's story was to unmask other highly placed spies, and perhaps rewrite history about the JFK assassination. There was more going on from day one than merely giving recognition to a deceased soldier of the Cold War.

Two weeks later I spoke to Jackie again. She had spoken to Bob Silvers, editor of the *New York Review of Books*, and to literary agent Mort Janklow. Silvers had seen her letter but had not had a chance to digest it and react. (I don't know if she ever followed through and spoke with Jann Wenner or Mike

Nichols, but I never saw her drop the ball on anything else.)

She again said, **"You'll end up as the hero of this in a Woody Allen story."**

I thought it was important to clarify whether I was backing into some sort of obligation or contract with Doubleday because of her many efforts. She assured me it was not the case, that Steve Rubin didn't want it and that she had told him of her personal interest in it. "I'm just doing it as me to help you, and for Leonid," she said. Again, her kindness and generosity with her time were absolutely amazing. And her interest in Leonid was obviously very, very strong. Moved by it all, I ran down the street to the florist and sent her a bouquet of flowers with a card reading, "Thanks again for your personal energies in this project." I intentionally sent a very modest bouquet since I figured any gushy excess would be a violation of the normality that she seemed to both crave and exude. It was the thought that counted.

Back came an absolutely lovely note from her together with the name of Paula Litzky, one of her friends she wanted to bring in to the project. She called Paula a very distinguished person who could help me a great deal. A couple days later on the phone

Paula explained that she had worked at Doubleday with Jackie until the previous June when she went independent. Jackie had discussed the project with Paula the previous week over tea. She thought Paula might be able to help identify an agent who knew both film and books. (The note and various other correspondence from Jackie are at Facebook.com/PhilMyersAuthor)

Paula surprised me by saying she had recently heard a lecture at Columbia University by Martin Malia, Nixon's advisor whose name had popped up as the source of "Uncle Curt's" knowledge of Leonid's group of conspirators. She called him a "real character, very secretive" but well respected as a Russia specialist. Then living in Europe, he was very smart and a very impressive speaker, although there is much controversy about what he says, she recounted.

We brainstormed a bit about how to handle organizing and marketing the project. She clearly knew her way around and was especially experienced in East Bloc publishing projects. She had brought to Jackie the manuscript of *The Last Tsar*, Jackie's best seller about the death of Tsar Nicholas II and his family. Jackie, she explained, was an "acquisitions editor," and did not get involved with many of the nitty gritty details of structuring a project. She's the one who spots good properties and acquires them for Doubleday. And her instincts had been very good, with a string of best-sellers including Michael Jackson's autobiography *Moonwalk* and Bill Moyers' book *Healing and the Mind*. Jackie sent me a copy of *The Last Tsar* with a note indicating that she thought I would enjoy it. Again, I was touched at her thoughtfulness and her focus on the project and me.

Soon I was on the phone with Jackie again. She had faxed to me a letter from super-agent Mort Janklow indicating that the story was very complex but that he'd be willing to look at it when the research and writing process was further along. "What we have here has the potential of a substantial true crime/espionage Soviet-American thriller but still needs to be structured and shaped." (Incidentally, Janklow is the agent who represented Pope John Paul II in obtaining a $6 million advance for his new book.)

She again recommended Paula as someone who knows a lot. "She's the bluebird in your backyard you don't think of," Jackie rhapsodized. And she especially urged me not to sell the story "for a song." I asked Jackie if she wanted to participate in personally debriefing Gulia when he visited New York. She saw no point in her doing it, since she wouldn't know enough about the story to contribute much to the questioning. But she added, "If I'm here I'd love to meet him." She also thought it would be useful to do a treatment, that is, a short summary of the story commonly used in the movie industry to sell movie ideas.

A couple of days later I spoke finally with Bob Silvers. If it could all be pinned down, the facts are so dramatic that any medium will go for it, he opined. Most of all he was interested in Gulia doing an article for the *New York Review of Books*. He thought it could be an article followed by a book, or possibly book excerpts in his publication.

We were now up to February 19, 1992 or less than two months after I first called Doubleday to reach Jackie. The week that changed everything was upon me.

In one dramatic week I:

a. found Leonid's children,

b. discovered that Leonid had made a secret trip to Russia in 1989 as part of the Iraqgate arms deal whereby the U.S. funneled cash to Saddam Hussein to buy weapons from Russia to use in his war with Iran,

c. identified likely intelligence operatives running the Metropolitan Museum of Art in New York where Leonid had worked,

d. started speculating on a possible tie-in of the Leonid murder to the JFK assassination, and

e. got the first bizarre anonymous phone call that seemed to suggest some connection between Leonid's death and something in the 60's.

With the clear linkage of Leonid's death to JFK's I really felt like I'd gone over the falls. There was no way to undo whatever I'd done, whatever that was.

## Chapter 13

### *The Music Tells the Tale*

I had sent Gulia a fax asking if he could help me find Leonid's children, Ilya and Irina, since Karl Katz had never called back.  I thought they might be able to give me access to Leonid's papers or notes, and Gulia had once said Leonid might have a code book of some kind.

I expected to find young Ilya in New York or Boston. But Gulia wrote back with the boy's address, sending the letter out of Russia with a trusted friend instead of communicating by any means that could be intercepted. I was shocked that Leonid's son was living in Santa Barbara. The coincidence was staggering that the young man should be attending Santa Barbara City College and living a few blocks from my research assistant, Joe the lifeguard.

Nineteen-year-old Ilya got a call from me out of the blue, and an invitation to dinner. I explained that I was doing some work both with an old friend of his father's and with Mrs. Onassis. Both had inquired about him, I said, so I wanted to give them the latest information about how he was doing. He happily agreed, and I invited Joe to join us so Ilya would have someone his own age who might make him feel more comfortable. Immediately I faxed Jackie that I had found the children and was going to have dinner with the son. (The daughter was married and living in Atlanta.)

Over dinner at the Harbor Restaurant out on Stearns Wharf, with a lovely view of the comings and goings of boats in the yacht-filled harbor, I told Ilya about my business efforts in Russia. He was fascinated and enthused about computer programming and bomb detectors and all the other Russian technology that I was planning to sell. I kept sprinkling in details about his father's past so that if he knew anything about the treason conspiracy he would know I was talking about it. But he showed absolutely no recognition of any of the details. Clearly, he had not a clue about his father's past. He had met Jackie, however, once or twice and recounted how his father had been good friends with her. He allowed how he should give her a call to keep in touch.

Horrors, I thought. The last thing I need is for Ilya to call Jackie and have her inadvertently spill the beans about Leonid's treasonous past and possible murder. It would be embarrassing for her and shocking for the boy. Since she had given me her home phone number, I called her first thing the next morning. We discussed the fact that the son obviously did not know, and she agreed that the decent thing was for me to tell him about his father's past as a Cold War hero. We thought that if the story came out later he would justifiably resent us having kept him in the dark. Although it entailed a risk that he would not be able to handle it or would leak the story some way deleterious to our project, it didn't matter. Telling him was the right thing to do. She volunteered to duck any phone calls from him in the meantime so that I could fill him in in person.

Immediately I called Ilya and invited him to my office on the pretense that I wanted to discuss my Russian businesses and how he could help. He eagerly came in the same afternoon. I explained that there was another Russian project, a book project. He listened raptly as I told the story of a small group of conspirators who had wanted to save the world from nuclear war. He was on the edge of his seat, loving every minute of it. And then I dropped the bomb: his father had been the ringleader.

The poor boy could hardly get out a coherent sentence for the next hour and a half.  But he immediately saw the possibility that the car accident in France had been murder. It turned out that his father's cousin, then living in Scranton, Pennsylvania had first responded to news of the death with the notion that it was murder. The children had dismissed his reaction at the time, even though the cousin had been arrested at the same time as their father in the Soviet Union. But now I had two totally unconnected sources, Karl Katz, via Jackie,  and Leonid's cousin, saying the same thing about the possibility of a murder. And there were some pretty strong indications that Leonid had been in the thick of something peculiar in New York up to his death.

Joe and I discussed all this on my phone, ignoring the presumed tap on it. Again, I thought I was likely to be safer if I let it be known what I was up to rather than trying to hide it. Trying to make sense of the increasingly weird coincidences and inferences, he and I brainstormed every possible scenario. These included Leonid as a plant in Mrs. Onassis's life for any of several reasons, and any tie-in to the JFK assassination. At that point, it never occurred to me that Jackie herself could have been a CIA agent. That possibility popped up much later but explained better some of her reactions. I'll deal with that notion in Chapter 31. I discovered that Gulia's friend, Vlad Zubock, was about to start going through the Communist Party Central Committee files in Moscow as part of a project coordinated through the Hoover Institute at Stanford. I asked him if he could get his hands on Leonid's file, and he thought he could (though he never did).

That's when the first anonymous call came. On February 28, 1992, I had just left for San Francisco when my secretary took down a bizarre message:

**"The music of the 60's is the same as the music in the late 80's, just remember that,"** said the anonymous man's voice. The caller hung up before she could even ask for a name.

I was totally baffled again. We had no events in the story either in the 60's or the late 80's, but I immediately wondered if someone meant to connect the deaths of JFK and Leonid. But Leonid died in 1990, not the late 80's, though his arms buying for Saddam and secretive trips to the USSR were in the late 80's. It didn't add up. Somebody seemed to be trying to tell me something, or signal that I should look further at something, but it was certainly not obvious what the message meant.

I called Gulia to ask if he knew who might have left such a bizarre message. He professed total ignorance, but in the oblique way we used to discuss delicate matters over the phone lines to Russia, he seemed to agree about it suggesting a link between the two deaths. Gulia was nobody's fool and not given to crazy speculation. If he thought the murders of JFK and Leonid were linked plausibly I had to take it very, very seriously.

Until and unless I had something more concrete, I resolved not to discuss this speculation with Jackie as yet. But I did brief Paula on it, and we discussed it many times in the future.

To cement things with Ilya a bit I took him as my guest to a Santa Barbara Committee on Foreign Relations dinner for Roy Huffington. A Texas oil and gas zillionaire, Huffington was George Bush's Ambassador to Austria. His son, Michael, was then married to Arianna Stasinopoulos Huffington who later founded the Huffington Post. Ilya handled himself nicely in the much older company, reflecting a polished upbringing in private schools in New York, and an old-world father.

I called Ilya and we met for coffee with Joe again. We discussed the anonymous call and the possibility that it connected his father's death with JFK's. He told how his father and Mrs. Onassis were very good chums. Ilya said that his father used to stop by her apartment often for coffee on his way home after work at the museum. That tidbit raised all kinds of questions in my mind about exactly how close, on a working or personal basis, the two had become.

Ilya also told us that many of his father's friends had been overwhelmingly FBI agents and people with intelligence pasts. One of the FBI people in his circle had simply disappeared for five years, then reappeared. Ilya told about going shooting with senior officials of the Met and his father, and that his father had confided that one of the very senior Met people (Philippe de Montebello, Chairman of the Board) who had been along for the day had an intelligence background.

By a wild coincidence, I discovered that so did another. One of my brothers had known him twenty-five years before when they were both in Venezuela. The Met official (its President, Bill Luers) had been a young intelligence officer involved in anti-Castro activity and known to my brother whose own background included military intelligence and teaching at West Point. To make it even wilder, this Met official, with an intelligence past, had been one of the speakers at the 1990 conference at the Council on Foreign Relations, where I met Vlad and started on the Russian adventure.

I told Ilya that Karl Katz was supposed to help me find him but had not done so. Ilya thought it was "bullshit" that Karl couldn't find him. He said that Karl knew all the people at the Met who knew his whereabouts, including the executor of his father's estate. It should have been exceedingly simple for him to find the kids and let me know where they were.

Ilya then told how his father had been able to leave the USSR thanks to the intervention of Senator Scoop Jackson (Democrat, Washington) with Soviet Premier

Brezhnev. An international committee, headed by Larry Wilson, a prominent antique arms collector, and current big-time arms dealer in New England, had agitated for the Soviets to give Leonid his exit visa. Ilya said Larry Wilson was friends with the people at the Met. Among Leonid's papers at his daughter's house I found a newspaper report of a reception for Leonid at Gracie Mansion, the New York Mayor's residence, with Senators Scoop Jackson, Jacob Javits, James Buckley, Warren Magnuson, and Congressman Joseph Biden. Clearly Leonid was not a country bumpkin.

Gulia had never mentioned anything about Leonid being involved with big name American politicians and anything other than museum work in the U.S. Leonid's fight for an exit visa from the Soviet Union had been an international cause célèbre. On July 13, 1972, the New York Times reported that Leonid had been dismissed as a curator at the Hermitage because he applied for an exit visa. He was much more than a museum curator, obviously. But what?

I wrestled with the question of what activities Leonid had been involved with in New York, long after the supposed end of the original plot in Russia. When is a museum curator not a museum curator, and a museum director not a museum director?  And when is a museum not a museum?

Nixon's White House Chief of Staff Bob Haldeman would answer that one for me later.

## Chapter 14

### *When Is A Church Not A Church?*

Trying to connect the dots and figure out what was happening was always best accomplished when I would swim my laps. My obsession with getting my swim daily seemed a bit odd, I'm sure, to Gulia. He explained that in Russia one could not simply waltz into any old public pool and jump in to do laps. The government required that you be certified to be in good health and without any heart problems. The City of Santa Barbara, I assure you, could care less if I am stupid enough to swim in the city pool with a weak heart. It's my own problem. Sink or swim. But the City of Leningrad would not allow such nonsense. I had to get an EKG and a certificate before I could use the pool Gulia had found for me.

So off we went to the medical clinic of the Academy of Sciences. Aha, I figured, now I'll see the fine care given to the privileged few. The Academy of Sciences, after all is roughly the equivalent of the entire U.S. Ivy League plus the national labs (like Lawrence Livermore Lab) combined. Its scientists surely had the best possible medical care, I imagined.

The building looked like a tumble-down stucco one-story garage. I was in shock. The medical equipment inside all looked like it was left over from World War II. I think it actually was. Indeed, they had an ancient EKG machine and the very sweet and charming and enormously fat woman doctor soon hooked me up. After an interminable period watching the creaky machine chart my heartbeat like a seismograph I had seen in college, she tore off the ten-foot-long paper graph. Gulia asked if I had passed, and she announced in bold tones, "Like a cosmonaut!"

I was good to go for a swim! Next stop, church. Yes, you read that right. Churches were not the Communists' favorite places. They tended to obliterate them one way or the other and to do everything they could to discourage religion. So, in downtown Leningrad, they simply dug a swimming pool inside one and turned it into my swimming nirvana.

Doing backstrokes looking up at the intact vaulted ceiling and fine decoration from about 1750, I thought it must be the most elegant pool on earth. It was an entirely different from the standard infinity pool, one that gave a sense of spiritual infinity. I swam the twenty-five meters between the pulpit and the nave, ecstatic at my surroundings. If ever sports had come close to a religious experience for me this was it. It combined my love of architecture with swimming and meditation.

Later I was heartbroken when Yeltsin gave the building back to the church and my pool closed. The fall of Communism definitely had one downside for me. But again, I had learned a great deal about the differences between life under the Soviets and the world I knew. The Soviets professed to care about the hearts of their people, but they tried to obliterate their souls. Yet in the process there was a certain comic opera character to the cultural mayhem and spiritual and literal slaughter.

I was literally swimming in absurdity.

# Chapter 15

## *Vlad and Sex Parties*

After checking with Gulia that it was OK to freely speak with Vlad, his protege who had been at Stanford with him, I decided to put my questions in front of him. Especially I wanted to focus on the anonymous phone call about the music of the 60's and late 80's. Vlad was passing through New York when I happened to be in Washington. I caught a plane to JFK Airport and took him to dinner at the La Guardia Marriott where I briefed him at length on the odd goings-on. Trying to give some historical context to it all, Vlad explained that under Eisenhower there had been almost no under-cover, back-channel communications between the U.S. government and Russia. Everything had gone through formal diplomatic channels. Under the Kennedy administration, all that changed dramatically. Especially he suggested I look at a book by historian Michael Beschloss detailing the unofficial communications between JFK and Khrushchev and focus on the relationship between JFK's brother Bobby and a Mr. Balshikhov. Well known as a KGB agent in Washington, Balshikhov met frequently with as a communications channel between JFK and

Khrushchev. He suggested that Balshikov and Bobby had been exceedingly "buddy-buddy," even enjoying sex parties together. The Beschloss book did not go that far in describing the relationship. But it said that the KGB and the FBI (under Bobby's formal control then) had built bridges, a dangerous activity that some, on each side, could have seen as treason, Vlad thought. And I imagined that FBI Director J. Edgar Hoover must have known and been livid about Bobby Kennedy and a KGB agent sharing hot babes.

Vlad also urged me to look at the spy history of Oleg Penkovsky, the CIA mole in Soviet military intelligence in the early 60's. If there was some connection that would pop up between the music of the 60's and that of the late 80's, he thought these would be important reference points. Vlad's comments certainly did not steer me away from the JFK/Leonid murder linkage theory. But it was still much too sketchy to take to Jackie, though I briefed Paula fully and left it up to her if she wanted to say more to Jackie. Vlad told me that he thought Gulia's motive in revealing all this may have been to establish me as a guarantor of his security. Vlad said Gulia was scared to death by the death of his old friend Leonid. If it had been KGB revenge for treason after all these years, then Gulia certainly had grounds to be scared. And if treason could prompt an execution on the Russian side of the equation, the Hoover and the ultra-right wing's perception of treason by JFK and his brother certainly could have prompted an execution in Dallas. There was no way to avoid looking at the symmetry.

In March 1992 Gulia and I took a long walk at midnight in Leningrad and discussed the Penkovsky case and all the curious information that I had discovered. I asked Gulia directly about his knowledge of any links between the JFK and Leonid deaths, and about the international committee that had agitated for Leonid's freedom. He said he knew nothing of it. It seemed that if I was going to uncover the whole story of Leonid, for Jackie and for myself, it would be necessary to aggressively go after sources other than Gulia.

If there was any doubt, however, about Gulia's prestige with the Americans it was dispelled by how they handled his daughter. She and her husband, both computer programmers, had decided to move to America and applied for green cards. Thinking that it was way too optimistic that they could get such visas, I told Gulia not to get his hopes up. He laughed and said, "No problem; it's already done." I couldn't believe my ears; computer programmers would not normally be eligible for instant green cards. I knew the situation well from doing my feasibility study for Typhoon Software.

The U.S. Consulate in Leningrad, however, had instantly given the couple "refugee status" and pushed it through. Gulia clearly had favors he could call in.

# Chapter 16

## *Haldeman Connects the Dots*

At the end of March, I decided to invite Bob Haldeman to the Santa Barbara Yacht Club for lunch. Bob, who was Nixon's former White House Chief of Staff, had heard me give a talk on the business aspects of my Russian ventures to the Santa Barbara Committee on Foreign Relations. Afterwards, he came up and suggested we have lunch someday to compare notes about our respective involvements there. He was a partner in a business center in Moscow at the Radisson Hotel from which Yelstin obtained a satellite phone to call President Bush during the 1991 coup. Haldeman moved to Santa Barbara after completing his Watergate-related prison sentence at the nearby Lompoc federal prison (where, ironically, I ended up myself in 2014).

Buying into the palmy chic of Santa Barbara's very expensive Hope Ranch suburb, where multi-acre home sites are standard and horses abound, he appeared to prosper. The neighbors included Essam Kashoggi, brother of a notorious arms dealer, Adnan Kashoggi, assorted movie stars, and the sister of the Shah of Iran. I first heard of him in town when he appeared as a consultant helping arrange financing for expansion of a retirement home on whose advisory board I served. Later I was serving on a community board looking into building a new performing arts center. Bob and his wife showed up on a VIP bus tour of a proposed site, a spectacular undeveloped ocean-view plateau owned by the Jesuits, and previously used only by hang-gliders. Since the lady who organized the tour was supposed to be bringing only potential heavy-hitter donors, I figured Haldeman must have been doing OK for himself. Certainly, the company he was keeping was not that of your average ex-con. Others on the tour included Katherine and Stewart Abercrombie (he had sold his elegant ranch to John Travolta and their current Montecito estate, with swans in the reflecting pool and hand-painted tiles by Goya around the fireplace, had twice been on the cover of Architectural Digest), Mrs. Milton Bradley Scott (he of the board game fortune) and Marcia Constance, whose family sold their oil business to Shell for a couple billion dollars.

What was so striking about Haldeman was how vigorous and youthful he seemed, although he was mid-sixties. With his hair grown out a bit from the White House era flat-top, he actually looked younger than my image of him from twenty years earlier. He could easily have passed for someone in his late forties. And he was relaxed, gracious, and almost chatty. Nothing remotely suggested the Nazi-like SOB that his critics portrayed him as during his White House tenure. And nothing suggested that he would die soon.

An offer from Haldeman to compare notes about our Russian activities, in light of my communications to Nixon, was just too remarkable to pass up.

Our rendezvous spot, the Santa Barbara Yacht Club, commands one of the most spectacular ocean-front sites in the world, built directly on the beach and sitting on pilings so that the occasional high wave can wash under the club and the many silver trophy cups, some of them three feet tall, in the upstairs display cases. From the second-floor dining room you gaze upon both the beach and hundreds of pleasure boats pincered between the steep slopes of the sun-drenched Santa Ynez Mountains, and the long curve of the breakwater, festooned with dozens of colorful flags. Tycoon and club member Max Fleischman, founder of the yeast company, built the breakwater as a gift to the city in the 1920's so that his huge yacht would be safe from storms. At that point, the club was already nearly 50 years old, one of the first on the West Coast. It's the ideal place to entertain when you need to make a good impression. When my wife organized the world premiere of Michael Douglas's movie "Romancing the Stone" as a charity benefit for UCSB, we had dinner with Michael at the Yacht Club to plan it. I joined when just out of law school and it was still primarily a sailor hangout with a bar, for after racing. Despite going more upscale over the years, installing full meal service, the nautical flavor is undiluted. Personally, I think the dining room is the most spectacularly beautiful places in the world to dine.

Despite its cachet, and its suitability for power lunches, it is the essence of California informality. The staff is "crew" and mostly friendly college students; everybody is on a first-name basis. Maître d' Dan Mead, with his charismatic smile and dazzling good looks seemed more like he should be playing love scenes with Julia Roberts (then rumored to be a new resident in town) than seating her.

It was at the Yacht Club I briefed Haldeman on the basics of the Leonid story. He was intrigued and volunteered that he would bring it up with President Nixon and get back to me. He and Nixon kept in touch, but Bob wanted to give some thought as to how exactly to open the subject with him. He thought he might start with some longtime Nixon staff people who had been with him back in the Vice-Presidential days.  But he clearly said that he'd pursue it and get back to me.

Haldeman thought Gulia's story made sense as it related to Nixon, as he knew that Nixon's old ties to the Communist world ran through France. He also announced out of the blue, to my amazement, that the Metropolitan Museum of Art in New York, the Getty Museum, and the National Gallery among others are frequently used as intelligence covers. I thought it was quite indiscreet of him, however helpful to me. I also figured that if a former White House Chief of Staff would discuss it openly it couldn't be exactly big news in the spy world.

Haldeman thought it was very odd that I had received no formal acknowledgement at all from Nixon of my previous communications to him in New Jersey. It was apparently standard practice, at least, to send some acknowledgement of written communications. He simply furrowed his brow and looked puzzled at Nixon's failure to respond directly to the communication.

I was very hopeful at first about what Haldeman might come up with. Especially I wanted him to fill in a gap in Gulia's story. Gulia had insisted that Leonid had a second channel open to Nixon when he was Vice President, apart from that through the French fencers. But he did not know who it was that gave Leonid direct access to Nixon. Leonid had never told him. And I still have never found out. It remains an enduring Cold War mystery. How was Nixon directly getting espionage information from the ringleader of a Soviet spy organization? Viscerally I think it was someone high in the Soviet government, someone who legitimately could communicate with the Vice-President of the United States, who was in cahoots with Leonid. But I can't prove it.

Although after that lunch I ran into him from time to time, Haldeman never got back with any response from Nixon, and I didn't push it. If Nixon again did not want to directly respond to me as he had not when I wrote to him at the outset of the adventure, I wasn't going to try to second guess him. But again, I had gotten from a close Nixon associate an important verification of part of the story. No less than a White House Chief of Staff had confirmed my suspicion that the Metropolitan Museum of Art was a hotbed of more than artistic activity, based on the spotty information I had about the peculiar backgrounds of some of its top leadership and the ties to arms dealing and the committee headed by Larry Wilson that agitated for Leonid's exit visa.

The last time I saw Haldeman was at a Santa Barbara Committee on Foreign Relations dinner, a few months later. McGeorge Bundy, JFK's National Security Advisor, was the speaker of the evening discussing denuclearization.

Haldeman seemed the picture of good health before dinner that night. As we walked in from the parking lot he confided that his Top-Secret clearance had recently been restored. It allowed him, he said, to get into government archives to work on a book he had in preparation. I was a bit baffled about why the government would do him any such favor, and why he'd make a point of informing me on the short stroll from the parking lot. But it didn't matter much, for only a few weeks later I returned from another Russia trip to discover that Bob was dead from a fast-moving cancer. I simply was baffled at how someone so vital could have declined so fast. I was also newly suspicious that perhaps his demise had been induced somehow. Bob died in November 1993. Nixon died in April 1994 just after a return from a trip to Russia, and Jackie died in May 1994. I was the only link between the three of them at that point, and I confess I found the coincidence unsettling.

## Chapter 17

### *I Meet Jackie in Person*

My first glimpse of her that day in May 1992, was from the elevator reception area high up in the Doubleday skyscraper, 666 Fifth Avenue. Visible from about 100 feet away, striding up the long corridor to retrieve me from the reception area, she was the essence of vigor.  Her friend, Paula Litzky, had warned me not to expect more than 15 minutes with her.  Paula's plan was to break-into the conversation to give Jackie a gracious excuse to end the meeting. But I certainly wasn't going to complain about "only" 15 minutes with the legendary First Lady.

The Doubleday building on Fifth Avenue was a fairly normal Manhattan skyscraper, distinguished only by the presence of Jacqueline Kennedy Onassis. (Today it is owned by the family of Jared Kushner, President Trump's son-in-law). Paula and I were to meet, at last, at the reception area on the 20th floor. As Jackie surged down the hallway I was immediately struck by the strength and fluidity of her movements.  She was like an athlete 20 years younger. She wore slacks and a sweater of comfort and taste, something unobtrusive and just right for the office. I was surprised at her brown wispy hair. From photos, I had always thought it looked more lacquered, but it seemed fairly natural. She led Paula and me to her office. Scott Moyers, a handsome WASP yuppie sort about 30 years old, was shoe-horned into a tiny space outside it. And the office itself was a big shock. I had envisioned something grand with parquet floors and museum quality paintings. Instead, it was tiny, dominated by what looked like an army-issued, Formica-topped desk.

I hesitated to put my Styrofoam coffee cup on her desk, but she said to go ahead, it wouldn't hurt it. I wanted to make my mark with her, I laughed, but not necessarily in the form of a stain on her desk. Every available surface of the modest space (albeit a corner office) was covered with books or papers. The floor was linoleum. Clearly this was a serious workspace of a serious editor. I was impressed.

I opened the discussion by saying I expected to return to Russia soon and would try to use audio cassettes to interview Gulia for several hours. Jackie was very concerned about the safety and prudence of doing so. She thought it should be done only outside Russia, that any such action would attract attention inside Russia. Surely, we couldn't even take a walk into the woods without being followed she said, and she thought my recording device would attract attention in customs. Later, with her advice ringing in my ears, I went out and bought a very generic Sony Walkman, but one with the unusual extra feature that it could record as well as play tapes. I figured a Walkman would not attract much attention being the ubiquitous music player of the times. She also urged me to keep it all very quiet. "You can't go to lunch and talk; people will even steal a new jogging book," she said.

Turning to a discussion of Leonid, she told how he was such a refined, old world gentleman. Dashing D'Artagnon of the Three Musketeers was his lifelong hero, and he was dressed as D'Artagnon in the photo on his final Christmas card in 1989. His daughter showed it to me. He spoke fluent French. He was completely charming. Then she stopped me cold by confessing, "I loved the man." The tone suggested a cultivated appreciation. But there it was nonetheless, whatever the full dimensions of the reality. After Onassis, before Templesman, Leonid clearly had greatly affected her. It was a point to be emphasized over and over by Paula's comments her conversations with Jackie about Leonid, and a lot of other little indicators, but most of all by my watching her react to the pictures of Leonid's French girlfriend.

Jackie returned to a discussion of the dangers of the project. She cited the James Angleton search for a CIA mole as an example of how we can't know who's doing what. "Every administration has its intelligence layers, stories that are dirty and would shock" she recounted.

I was shocked to have her bring up Angleton. Head of CIA counterintelligence during the JFK years, Angleton had ripped apart the CIA searching for a KGB mole. In 1964, just after the JFK assassination, a Soviet defector, KGB agent Yuri Nosenko, claimed to have seen Oswald's file and that the Russians had nothing to do with the assassination. Angleton locked him up and tried to break him. Furthermore, he never let Nosenko talk to the Warren Commission openly. Angleton never believed Nosenko's information was legitimate and that his insistence of the Soviet Union's innocence was completely untrustworthy. Angleton was eventually removed and Nosenko's legitimacy generally accepted. If, however, Angleton was right and Nosenko was sent as a bogus defector, it certainly meant the issue of KGB participation in the JFK assassination was a live one. There was simply no doubt that by bringing up Angleton in the context of our research into Leonid's death and his spy plot, Jackie was opening the question of a Russian role in JFK's assassination and whether there was some overlap between the two events. In that first meeting in her office, thus, it was very clear that we were dealing with something potentially far more vast than a 1950's network to warn of nuclear attack. And she was gung-ho to pursue it.

Remarkably, the father of the real KGB mole, Rick Ames, who was arrested in 1993, had worked once for Angleton. Later we discovered that it was quite possible Ames had been arrested because our research into Leonid's death pointed directly at Ames as the intelligence leak. But again, I get ahead of myself. Simultaneously with our research, the CIA was frantically looking for a mole inside who had betrayed several agents that had been liquidated.

Jackie also speculated that the French might not want the Leonid story, with the link through French fencing and intelligence, to come out. It might involve other things they don't want discussed, she thought. At that point, the French intelligence services had not yet acknowledged their mistake in killing the wrong persons in the staged car crash of

1964. And Princess Di's death by car crash in France had not occurred.

And she also feared that my Haldeman contact with Nixon could result in a "shutdown" of the project. She disdained Haldeman as a "felon," and conveyed a very real moral revulsion. When I raised the possibility of seeking an interview with Nixon she recoiled with horror and was adamant in her opposition to that idea. I decided not to cross her and avoided any further Nixon contact.

I told her that I appreciated her caution; it served as a plank hitting me between the eyes. But I intended to barge ahead, trying all the while to identify risks so that I knew which risks were acceptable and which were not.

We looked at next steps for the research, including going to Leonid's cousin in Pennsylvania, Israel Schmooker. He was supposedly in on the original plot, and the only person I knew of outside Russia who could discuss it from first-hand knowledge. We agreed it would be best to hold off until we could better define the scope of the story. Again, that reasoning made it clear to me she was thinking about the Russian role in the JFK assassination from day one of our collaboration.

We were not sure what kind of reception I would get from the cousin, who was said to be a difficult character. Jackie scoffed at Leonid's son Ilya's doubts about Karl Katz in not helping me find Leonid's children. She said that he was a dear friend, active in Jewish causes and would help any Jew anywhere any time. She could not conceive of him being engaged in anything shady. But I was much less certain knowing the company he was keeping at the Metropolitan Museum of Art in New York, and his disregard of his commitment to help me find Leonid's children. For once I thought Jackie was being the naïve one.

Paula and Jackie discussed the need and difficulty of finding a trustworthy writer. They thought it was too early, and I should first see what else I could get out of Gulia, then write up my notes. It seemed to them there were two stories: the Russian spy story and my own about how I got involved in the whole thing. I thought they were right and agreed and the idea of this book was born.

I told Jackie that it seemed odd to me, also, to be dealing with Haldeman. When I was in college, during Watergate, he had been the devil incarnate to me, whereas, I told her, "I always liked you." She seemed to appreciate the comment and asked if

Haldeman still had his short, funny hair, gesturing flat across her head. In fact, he had grown it out a bit and looked quite dashing for his age, I said.

Gorbachev, the last premier of the Soviet Union, now retired, I noted, was possibly going to buy a house in Santa Barbara. My daughter's godfather, Marty Mielko, a realtor, had told me Gorbachev had made an offer on a $20 million super-estate in Montecito, the ritzy suburb. Mielko was involved tangentially and had consulted me about some details of doing business with Russians, particularly how to get the money from Russia into a California escrow account.

She was fascinated, saying, "I feel like I'm in on a secret" and that she was going to meet Gorbachev soon at the Kennedy library in Boston. I mentioned the Gorbachev situation to Gulia later as well. Apparently, he was horrified and mentioned it to an old friend, a bishop in the church and told the bishop that Gorbachev's money could not possibly be clean. The church didn't sell.

When I mentioned that Leonid's daughter had told me she remembered her father meeting with Nixon and Kissinger after they came to the U.S., Jackie said that Gorbachev would be well-advised to do as Kissinger had done. He "wanted to live higher on the hog," she laughed, and had hired bodyguards to make him look more important.

I felt it important to say to Jackie directly that I did not want the project to be a source of any distress to her personally. I expressed my concern about the sensationalist distortions that could come from her involvement with such a project. She explained that she thought the book should come out first in order to maintain the integrity of the story. Clearly, she had faith in the printed word and felt that as long as the record was accurate in print, she didn't care what Hollywood did with it. They would do whatever they wanted anyway, she said. And she was utterly dismissive of the movie industry. I felt very strongly my obligation to repay her kindness by writing something totally accurate.

I then raised with her what I thought was one of the most sensitive subjects and one which I feared might cause her to opt out of the project. It struck me that someone for unknown reasons might want to manipulate either myself, or her, into bringing this story to the world's attention. I decided it was important to point out my concerns very directly. We agreed that it was impossible to be sure of anything. It was possible that this was an effort to discredit the KGB by showing their ineptness, and/or the impossibility of shutting down a society, as the Communists had tried to do. Who exactly had what hidden agenda here was a very murky question.

I told Jackie that the book was still far from my primary business activity, and that not only was it a story but its discovery and unveiling were a fascinating chapter of my life. Sometimes it was more interesting to continue with my own process than to worry about the demands of keeping the project under wraps. If I stumbled and let out the story accidentally during the research process I could accept it. Jackie referred to my "verve," but tempered it with a French quote she thought fit my "damn the torpedoes" aspect of charging ahead with the story: "Il a les défauts de sa caractère" (He has the faults of his character).

She was both astute, and bluntly honest. If the quote seemed like an implicit criticism of me to my face, it was also an existential acceptance of someone being who they are and a curious and unique kind of acceptance. To me it suggested her attitude towards other key men in her life and how she viewed their characters and shortcomings and coped with them.

After 90 minutes it was time for her to head off for lunch.   She had maintained eye contact with me throughout the meeting. And far from being a lightweight, she had been virtually verbal-aggressive, keenly analytical, and quite thoroughly professional. I was even more impressed with her in person than I had been on the phone. I thanked her profusely for her generosity of time and her attention and kindness. She said I didn't owe her a thing. "It's an adventure," she gushed, as she swirled around putting on her full-length black leather coat with the *Searle* label. And in that moment, I was astonished to be part of an adventure for this remarkable woman who surely had seen it all. I was thrilled with our rapport and the way we had been thrown together to deal with questions that mattered to her profoundly. I felt even more strongly that I had a real friend.

We walked to the elevator and went down together. She popped on her signature big sunglasses and melted into the crowd on Fifth Avenue, while Paula and I went off to the Peninsula Hotel for lunch and to debrief.

Paula explained to me that Jackie did, indeed, want to do the book if there were no "blowups" and it were fully researched and packaged. Paula and I agreed that if any bombshells emerged, such as JFK assassination issues, I would run them by her first.

At that point I told Paula of Vlad's comments about Balshikhov and Bobby Kennedy having sex parties, and that I was looking into the history of the Penkovsky and Popov affairs. Penkovsy and Popov were CIA moles in Soviet intelligence before and after the Leonid episode. About Penkovsky there is a recent book called *The Spy Who Saved the World*, reciting how his primary function had been the same as Leonid's group, i.e., to give advance warning of a Soviet first strike. His intelligence about the poor state of Soviet missile forces was critical in JFK's decision to face down the Soviets in the Cuban Missile Crisis.

I also told Paula I had informed Jackie previously about the link between the Metropolitan Museum official, Bill Luers, and the anti-Castro efforts in Venezuela. She was quite surprised that Jackie was still "in" after that one. Clearly Paula thought it was getting all too close to the JFK assassination-related subjects. There is an enormous body of discussion about whether the efforts under the JFK administration to assassinate Castro had led to a counter-effort to assassinate JFK. So anything that tied together our Leonid story with the CIA's anti-Castro efforts caused red lights to flash in Paula's mind.

Paula also explained that Jackie had a "real tough side."  After the terror of JFK's assassination in 1963, where she had to wonder "where did this event come from, and how could she protect her children," she had survived absolutely the worst.

A couple of weeks later Paula faxed me a list of suggestions on how to go about interviewing Gulia and organizing my thoughts and notes.  She said she had talked to Jackie about some of the information I gave her on the Penkovsky history.  I had noted that the Penkovsky operation was presumed to have emanated from anti-Khrushchev forces inside Russia that wanted to expose Khrushchev's vulnerabilities, have him humiliated and removed. If that sounded a lot like Leonid and his group's disdain for Khrushchev, you're right. Certainly, it made sense that people in the Soviet nuclear program might have enlightened or befriended its director, KGB chief Laurent Beria. When Stalin died, Beria started some Gorbachev-like reforms, including ending some of Stalin's attacks on Jews (the famous "doctors plot") that many feared were leading to new pogroms, i.e. repressions and arrests of Jews.

Khrushchev and his pals had arrested Beria after he had led the USSR for only six months and assassinated him (a mere ten years before the JFK assassination), dooming themselves to be seen as dangerous morons by many in the nuclear priesthood. Between Vlad's comments about Bobby Kennedy, Balshikov, and Penkovsky, and the clash of Beria and Khrushchev loyalists, clearly there were big and lethal forces in play in Leonid's story.

Paula's reaction to the expanding tentacles of the Leonid story and her discussion of it with Jackie was clear. Paula wrote to me: "I am afraid now she (Jackie) sees me at the bottom of the same can," referring to the famous "squished in a trash can" comment of Jackie's.

But Jackie, said Paula, was gripped by the story of the spies and the ringleader who had died. Mrs. Onassis's vigorous intellect and intense curiosity kept things rolling. She wanted to debrief me about everything I had discovered so far about her friend, Leonid, ringleader of the group Gulia had told me had wanted to warn the West of a nuclear first strike by the Soviets. And she wanted to know especially about his French girlfriend in the 1950's. I was clearly going to be asking Gulia more about his comments that Leonid had had quite a fling with the young French fencer.

Over the course of that first hour and a half meeting with Jackie, I felt that we had started a bonding process. We would explore the suspicious death of a man she announced to me that day that she had loved. It began to make sense why she was so gripped. It was more than a Cold War espionage story, a potential bestseller, or a recent murder; she had suffered an intensely personal loss and wanted to know its cause.

And she had not known he was a spy until I brought her the story (or so she claimed). Then she had first raised the possibility that he had been murdered, before it even crossed my mind.

If I was going to navigate my little boat through this situation I was going to have to be sure the bow was turned into the waves to avoid capsizing, as I learned in the sailing club at Stanford. The potential to get swamped here was obvious.

In those first 90 minutes in her presence, what had struck me most of all were her piercing, elegant, intelligent eyes. No one I've met before or since, whether lover, coworker or interrogator, has ever sustained eye contact as intensely with me as she had done. I walked away feeling strongly that it was much more than just a curious acquisitions editor

getting a briefing on a possible book project.
Something had passed between us.
Somehow, I was now part of her world.

I suppose I shouldn't have been surprised
the first time a male friend asked me if I'd
slept with her. But the more it happened, the
more shocked I was. Their imaginations were
not dampened, of course, as my circle of
friends found out about my subsequent
meetings at her apartment. It was ridiculous;
but people kept asking and it told me a lot
about the misperceptions of her that she had
to block out.

I was thrilled to be working with Jackie
on a project for exactly the same reason I later
wanted to hire Jerome, the waiter at the Hotel
du Cap-Eden-Roc. It became apparent that
she understood what it took to bring order to a
little bit of the cosmos that was under her
control. It could take the form of organizing
material for a book or organizing a life.

On a later visit I saw the view from her
penthouse's library window onto Central Park.
There was a similarity to the view from the
terrace at the Hotel Du Cap-Eden-Roc, of the
Azure Coast. It seemed like the gods had
favored her with calm and beauty in an urban
cove surrounded by skyscraper hilltops. But in
her case, we all know what chaos she endured

to get to that calm haven. Whatever chaos below might send ripples towards her perch where she had a view of perfection, the waves could not reach high enough to reach her in her Penthouse.  The butler's starched white jacket, like Jerome's, didn't hint at the danger or disorder he was ready to handle, if somehow some chaos reached as high as her terrace. But his martial arts skills could handle it (or me). I hoped nothing in his brain registered, even for an instant, DANGER due to my behavior.

I knew that her instincts spotted danger in a flash. The first time we spoke about Gulia and Leonid's history of self-appointed world-saving espionage, she spent 20 minutes grilling me on how I had found out about the story.  That's when she had announced, in words burned forever into my brain and soul,

**"You're going to end up squished in a trash can."**

I was finding out constantly a lot more about where she thought there was danger.

Indeed, Jackie's sunglasses were oversized, just like in so many photos from the tabloids. Whether she was on shopping binges in the Greek Isles, or Paris, or carrying out official duties as First Lady, she had so often worn those trademark glasses.  But I had only a glimpse of her in them as she tossed them on when we exited the elevator at Fifth Avenue. It was her eyes I had enjoyed for the past hour and a half.

She headed up Fifth Avenue anonymously.

I was frankly astonished that photographers weren't there snapping pictures of Jackie Onassis and me as we emerged from the Doubleday Publishing offices. After all, the tabloids had somehow managed once upon a time to photograph her sunbathing naked in a private Mediterranean cove, like Greta Garbo had done with Jane Fonda. She was fair game anywhere, any time. Her face sold magazines worldwide. But I had seen the eyes behind the glasses. No photographer could show me anything about Jackie she hadn't revealed herself to me.

## Chapter 18

### *Check It Out And Tell Jackie*

I decided it was time to see if I could get any information about Larry Wilson, the arms dealer who had organized the international committee to pressure the Soviets to let Leonid leave. But I wanted to do so very quietly. I thought I would bounce the problem off an old buddy, Mark, who had worked for the Office of Naval Intelligence and had been a Navy Seal in Vietnam. I figured he would have some ideas of how to go about a background check, so I sent him a letter outlining my problem. I knew I could count on his discretion.

What I didn't count on was him doing the check himself. A few days later he called me in a very excited state. He confessed that he had asked one of his Navy Seal friends, who was now in operations in one of the top U.S. intelligence agencies, to check Larry Wilson's name. Mark shocked me with the information that "he runs some drug money and guns over the border in Southeast Asia." Furthermore, "He's nobody, but he's being used." "You can't trust him," and "He has a lot of garbage he's carrying around." "He thinks he's an operative," but "He's being used, a 'patty melt,' 'cheese on top of the hamburger'," and "Lots of people would like to see him gone." Obviously, Mark's comments are only hearsay and I cannot say anything about the truth of them. It's certainly possible that Mark was being used to disseminate some disinformation to me. But I hung up the phone in disbelief, again thinking about getting squished in a trash can. Many years later Larry Wilson was doing prison time for some kind of gun deal gone bad, or maybe because someone succeeded in getting rid of him as they were later to try to do with me.

I wrote to Jackie with this information, and the scoop about the people at the Met having intelligence backgrounds, all of whom I figured she knew. I also told her finally about the anonymous call to my office ("The music of the 60's is the same as the music in the late 80's, just remember that!") and speculated that Leonid had been part of some ongoing intelligence operation during his years in New York, possibly even a continuation of the 1950's early warning plot or something even more dramatic.

What I couldn't understand was why delicate information kept falling into my lap. As I wrote to Jackie, "I think I must be very much on the lookout that someone is trying to manipulate me (or through me, you???) into revealing something." Such frankness with her, I was afraid, might cook my goose. You didn't have to be a rocket scientist to understand the subject of revelations she might be able to make, and just what I was referring to, especially after our Angleton/Nosenko conversation. At that point, it was obvious to me that anyone trying to manipulate information about Jackie had to be assumed to have some kind of link to Dallas.

And Jackie, frankly, had shown herself to be every bit as smart as a rocket scientist. Surely the project was simply getting too hot for her to be involved I thought and dreaded.

Would she withdraw from the project, I wondered? Had it gotten into territory that was too delicate?  Not at all; but after my letter she called again and said to me: "**I think it's dangerous**."  She told me that when she read my letter she thought to **herself "Jeepers, I just have to tell this man to hold this close to your chest."** She voiced a concern that I was too naïve.  But far from telling me to drop it, or that she was bailing out, she noted that Paula was a straight arrow and that I should "**try to sign it up before someone else does."** The acquisition editor's instincts were all in gear.  I really had to laugh at the parallel to my own first response to the story in Russia and expressing that I thought it was a Tom Clancy-type material worthy of a movie. Not being quite so naïve as Jackie feared, of course, I had signed up Gulia long before. Nobody was going to do the story without me.

I also brought up a new subject to Jackie to see if she would be interested in a completely different book topic: parapsychology.  At the urging of one of my clients, I had asked Gulia if we could get our hands on secret KGB research into parapsychology.  One day my client had been sitting in my office as I regaled her with the latest wild stories about my Russian adventures.  In had come a fax from Gulia asking if I could run down a rumor that the U.S. Air Force wanted to buy some MIG 31's for target practice.  First, I did a little research and couldn't find any reference to a MIG 31 even existing. It seemed like it would have to be a new model. I was dumbfounded by the request, it not being anywhere even remotely like anything I had ever done.  (I did manage to get a recently-retired Air Force General to pass it along to the Joint Chiefs of Staff, but by sheer dumb luck. He was a friend of my pal, Henry Huglin, from the Committee on Foreign Relations.)  As we were laughing at the "anything goes" tenor of my stories, my friend said while I was at it I should get the KGB's research into parapsychology.  Why not, we laughed.  And then I got serious.  My friend, Ness Carroll, told me about a best-seller a few years ago entitled  P*sychic Discoveries Behind the Iron Curtain*. There had been many rumors in the West that the Soviets had done a lot of work in the fields of ESP and related paranormal phenomena.  I figured that if Jackie were interested in a book on the subject, I'd give it a shot. So, I asked Jackie if she would be interested in it as a book subject if we could get the material.  She was quite enthusiastic. This led to me sponsoring a three-day conference in Leningrad at which the KGB released many research papers that previously had been classified. Among the topics offered to us were a project to see if Shamans in Siberia using telepathy could communicate with cosmonauts in space in the event of a radio failure. And my favorite paper that was offered (though we didn't accept it) was "The role of the scientist in psychoterror." Psychoterror was a set of techniques to keep hostile populations under control, whether dissidents or conquered nations.

## Chapter 19

### *"You're In Deep But Nobody's Going To Hurt You"*

Next, who should drop in to Santa Barbara but Gorbachev. He arrived on the Malcolm Forbes private jet (painted money green) direct from Moscow to visit retired President Ronald Reagan at his ranch. From Santa Barbara he went to San Francisco where he made several appearances. Through George Doubleday I had met Jim Garrison, the head of the Gorbachev Foundation in the U.S., so I was invited to go see Gorbachev. How could I resist, especially if he might end up as my neighbor in Santa Barbara?  He gave a curiously unpolitical speech, more of a moral homily.  It was entirely different from what I had expected.

From there I was off to Leningrad to see Gulia again, my Sony Walkman on my hip. Jackie was wrong, or at least I was sufficiently clever in my choice of recording devices.  No one in customs seemed to notice, or at least care about, my Walkman/recorder.

As usual, my visit was a whirlwind tour of scientists, secret labs and the Communist faithful turned entrepreneur.  I was busy trying to figure out how to build a company around a technology for detecting plastic explosives in luggage.  And on this trip Gulia got me into the secret lab to see the prototype and "play" with explosives and the bomb detection machine.

I was impressed enough by his ability to get me through the door. But it was nothing compared to what was coming next. As we drove away from the explosives detection lab he told me he wanted to show me another secret lab.  This one built shock absorbers for buildings, and the scientists hoped to be able to sell them now in California for earthquake mitigation for skyscrapers. A light went on in my head, and I asked why they had been developing such things in Leningrad, where there was no history of earthquakes. Gulia chuckled and explained.

The shock absorbers had been designed for placement under military command and control structures, so that they could survive nuclear blast. No way would I be permitted to see the shock absorbers in an actual installation. They were too secret. I laughed and asked Gulia how many signatures and how many days it would take to get me in this door of this lab. He chuckled again and said that no amount of signatures could get me in the door. We would just go in anyway. The director of the institute would come down and wave the security people away from the door, and we would simply never officially have been there.

My heart stopped. Visions of wintering in a Siberian prison camp flashed through my head. If I went in would I ever come out? As always seemed to be the case, every time I thought my Russian adventure couldn't go over the top any more, it did.

I almost told him to pack it in and I'd head home. Plane schedules ran through my head. But again, I figured I had bet on my horse, and I'd stick with him. Gulia hadn't steered me wrong yet, and the sheer experience of working with him was an endless thrill. So off we went to the shock absorber lab, and sure enough, it all happened as he said it would. During our visit, I saw film of buildings surviving an actual nuclear blast. The institute's director sent them home with me.

The big metal gates not only swung open to let me in, but to let me back out again, as well my confidence in Gulia's extraordinary talents and connections was renewed.

Finding time to do the interviews about the spy plot was a problem, as Gulia took very seriously his mission to help convert the defense industry and technology to peaceful uses. But one evening Gulia's family gathered at his daughter's apartment for a birthday party. And I seized my chance. We escaped to his granddaughter's bedroom and the tape started running. There was much that Gulia specifically wanted to get recorded. He seemed quite relieved to get it out of his head and into someone else's medium.

Once we were done, however, I started wondering again if I was crazy to be doing all this. With Jackie's comments still ringing in my ears about how the interview was sure to attract attention, I kept looking for any signs of our being followed. Out the window I couldn't spot any suspicious cars or pedestrians below the apartment. I certainly wasn't trained for, or interested in, the twisted mindset of the espionage game. Jackie was right: we Americans don't live in that paranoid way, as did the citizens of the Soviet Union. But Gulia's brashness seemed to indicate that he, too, did not live in a paranoid way. Again, it struck me as remarkable how his spunk and brashness had survived the totalitarian superstate.

Only the fact that Gulia's entire espionage story was ancient history seemed to make it reasonable for me to pursue. I figured that since I wasn't dabbling in current transmission of secrets or plots, I was probably pretty secure. Most comforting, in some ways, was that Gulia seemed blissfully ignorant of Leonid's activities in New York and of the company he had kept there. If Leonid had been up to some sort of mischief, it didn't seem to involve anything that could threaten me in Russia. (This position ended up being tragically simplistic as I explain in the final chapters).

Still, at one point I felt that I should go out of my way to be sure Gulia understood that I was not an agent of any kind, not CIA, not DIA, not NSA, not FBI, only JD (a law degree). Gulia just shrugged off my protestation and said, "What difference would it make?" I had to let that comment sink in. He was utterly indifferent if I was an American intelligence agent. What did that say about the course of events? At the time I shrugged my shoulders and thought that he maybe it was right. In my ultimate interpretation of the subsequent events, I always came back to that comment to try to make sense of everything.

My departure through Russian customs had me holding my breath. They routinely X-ray all luggage both when entering and leaving the country (twice when leaving). Old-timers had told me that departures used to include detailed searches of all luggage. I kept wondering what would trigger such a thing on that particular day. The interview tapes were tucked in my jacket pocket. But nobody checked anything in detail. I simply waltzed on through and jumped on the shuttle bus to the plane. As my Delta flight to Frankfurt lifted off, I applauded and gasped, surprised at the strength of my own reaction to my safe departure. I couldn't wait to brief Jackie on the new information.

On June 3, 1992 I faxed Jackie with more details about the story. It was a juicy number. I went into great detail on the original spy plot and commented that there were no post-1962 bombshells because Gulia knew nothing about the circumstances of Leonid's departure for the

West and his activities in New York. I also wrote (in French, because occasionally we chatted in French) that I had been very astonished by my reaction to Gorbachev in San Francisco. I had expected someone cynical and diabolical, and finally I had concluded that he resembled more a philosopher or a professor, someone of principle and a formidable wisdom.

On June 10, 1992 I followed it up with a mind-bender fax to Jackie again, after speaking to Mark, the old Navy Seal. I had called to ask for his opinion of what Leonid's 1989 secret trip to Russia with a bogus passport could possibly have been about. Not wanting to slip into too much paranoia, I wanted to see if he thought it had all the hallmarks of a covert intelligence operation. Mark, I figured, could provide a reality check.

He said he wanted to think it over for a day, but again he charged ahead without asking me and called someone, I know not whom. Mark called me back in a wild frenzy. He sounded drunk. Leonid, he said, had been on a secret mission. He said I was "in deep," and that I was "not good enough to handle anything more." He said I was viewed "as a lightweight" (by whom, for God's sake, I wondered, and of course I was not trained as an agent of any kind!!). He confirmed that my phone was tapped and alluded to the anonymous call about the music of the 60's and 80's as apparently being from the "boys." "You're in trouble, but nobody's going to hurt you," he ranted. He said I had stumbled into something and there was no way to straighten it all out. I could do what I want "over there, but not here." He said I should "back off" and that I wasn't going in the right direction, that I was missing everything."

"Somebody screwed up major and sent the poor asshole (Leonid) in to find out what they had," he blurted. Again, the suggestion was obvious that Leonid had been murdered.

The next day Mark called back, sober and all business. He recommended that the best way to avoid problems was to bring in an investigative reporter. That way, he explained, the intelligence services will keep their hands off. I noted the curiosity of the advice about bringing in an investigative reporter neatly matched what Jackie, and Paula, had suggested.

Immediately I copied all my material and dispersed it to multiple locations with instructions to the recipients that if anything should happen to me the materials should be sent to *Los Angeles Times* reporter Doyle McManus. Doyle and I knew each other from freshman year at Stanford when we both wrote for the *Stanford Daily*.

Always assuming the "boys" from NSA/CIA/FBI or somewhere similar were listening, I also spoke about my actions freely on the phone. And of course, I recounted the conversation with Mark, in toned-down terms, in my June 10 fax to Jackie.

I also told Jackie several details I had learned from Leonid's daughter, including that Leonid, once in the U.S., had met several times with Nixon and Kissinger, not what museum curators usually do. Most explosively, I added that shortly before his death Leonid had made a secret trip to the USSR using a bogus passport supplied by an associate of Larry Wilson based in Helsinki. I said that the last item per Mark "has resulted in a lot of bells and whistles blowing and red lights flashing." Apparently, I have hit a nerve, and the not-too-gentle suggestion has come through a reliable source that I occupy myself with "pursuing anything but that information while the dust settles."

Now that I had three sources indicating Leonid had been murdered, I was much more concerned that Jackie would finally dump the project and run for the hills. I was ecstatic instead when on June 12 she faxed me a handwritten note referring to my June 3 and 10 research reports I had faxed to her saying, **"Your faxes are intriguing and that is an understatement. Thanks so much for sending them."** She was absolutely along for the whole ride. It was an incredible rush, the most intense of my life.

I was delirious that Jackie had been both so attentive to and impressed with my faxes that she took the time to let me know of her strong reaction. It had almost a healing quality, touching me deeply. In showing her reaction to me and thanking me, it seemed some qualitative change had occurred in the freedom in our relationship. Sending the blunt faxes, I had thought, was pushing the bounds of the license I had in communicating with her and was clearly counter to the limitations Paula had tried to impose. To be rewarded with spontaneous and obviously very sincere thanks, totally beyond the bounds of anything called for by any protocol or norm of communications between us, provided a rush of acceptance. We were not yet on a first-name basis, but it felt like something had changed. It was a tremendously satisfying moment of connection. I savored it and was excited by the acceptance, and by her, in a way I had never been before.

On June 15 Paula also told me on the phone that Jackie had been "turned on" by my faxes.

Life is strange.

The concern about someone trying to manipulate me into revealing something continued to nag me. To cover myself, I also wrote to the Justice Department to ask, for the second time since my Russia efforts began, about compliance with a law requiring agents of foreign governments to register. I gave them a summary of my experience and asked for their opinion of the applicability of the law governing registration of agents of foreign governments. I told them that it was possible some foreign government (though I could not be sure which one) might be trying to influence the Congressional Iraqgate investigation about arms purchases for Saddam Hussein, or other U.S. government decisions through me. I was not about to leave open any loophole for the U.S. government to charge that I had acted surreptitiously in conjunction with any unfriendly aliens. Whatever was going on, I had no intention of becoming its victim.

The Justice Department, which previously had corresponded with me on similar points about doing business with Russia, never responded to my letter which I found extremely peculiar since the first time I wrote they responded quickly.

June 22,1992, I headed to New York to meet with Jackie again and to deliver the transcripts of my extensive interviews of Gulia. I also had in hand several photographs of Leonid and the French fencers, including the girlfriend. If there was ever a moment that it crossed my mind someone might try to stop me, it was then. Once the transcripts were in Jackie's hands, there would be no way to shut it down, even by getting rid of me. And I doubted anyone would have the gall to try to get rid her. At least that's what I thought then. When she died at the age of 64 a little less than two years later, after a surprisingly swift decline due to a form of cancer (like Bob Haldeman), I had to rethink whether someone had wanted to shut us down by disposing of her. Whatever I would come out and say about the Russian links would have nothing like the weight that any pronouncement from her would have.

From the plane, an hour out of New York, I decided to call Joe, the lifeguard-turned-research-assistant, about something totally different. He was breathless, having received a bizarre phone call just after I left. No one spoke, but for five minutes there were

Gregorian chants playing on his phone before the other party hung up. "The music of the 60's is the same as the music of the late 80's" came back to mind. Could the latest odd call mean that the music referred to in the first anonymous call pointed at the Catholic Church? Was it the common thread in the deaths of JFK and Leonid?

Again, the call had come just after a research breakthrough as I was trying to piece things together and decide on a next step and as I was setting out to see Jackie.

Just before I left to see Jackie we had we definitively identified the Ukrainian Catholic cellmate of Leonid in Siberia in the 1950's as Bishop (later Cardinal) Josef Slipyj. The call seemed to confirm our research, and the Catholics had to figure in to the whole story more prominently than I had realized. We now had some sort of covert mission in the late 80's that apparently included the Catholic Church. Soon I would find out that the church was apparently laundering money to buy arms in Russia for Iraq. The puzzle was fitting together. Or at least someone wanted me to think so!

To my astonishment, Scott Moyers had called and asked if I could meet Jackie at her apartment instead of the office. Paula was to join us as well. Paula shocked me by saying I should assume that Jackie's apartment was bugged. I wasn't sure if it was a none-too-subtle way of letting me know I'd better behave, or if Jackie was doing a Nixon-like thing and taping her office conversations. It didn't really matter either way. So dutifully I arrived at 4:30 p.m., transcripts and photos in hand. I rode up in the wood-paneled elevator to her 15th floor penthouse where she greeted me almost as I stepped off. But *was* Jackie's penthouse really bugged, I wondered?

## Chapter 20

### *San Francisco Seal*

Before going to her home the first time, I met with Mark the Navy Seal in San Francisco. I decided that I wanted to see him eyeball to eyeball to find out if he could flesh out his wild comments about Leonid's secret mission. He had been very nervous about speaking on the phone, so I flew him to the City.

First, we had lunch at the Hyatt overlooking Union Square. I explained much of what I had been up to, from the Typhoon subs on. He seemed greatly relieved to learn that I was not dealing in arms or anything illicit. When Mark had made his latest phone call, he said, the information had popped out that I was on the CIA "hot sheet." It flagged me as someone to watch on overseas journeys to determine if I was secretly in the arms trade. He also thought that the dubious distinction had arisen since the first checking up he did on Larry Wilson. No wonder, I thought, if somebody thinks I'm linked somehow to such a character as Larry Wilson. Between the Typhoon submarine telexes and Larry Wilson, I wasn't surprised to be put on some list.

I had absolutely positively made it a rule not to deal in anything that involves selling arms, so that one was easy to dispel. Early in my days of travelling to Russia a friend in Santa Barbara had asked me to meet with some businessmen who wanted to buy helicopters from Russia. It wasn't something I knew anything about, but as a courtesy to my friend I took the meeting. When it turned out they were talking about military helicopters, i.e. weapons, I shut the meeting down fast. I asked them if they had the necessary arms-dealing license from the US State Department and said I absolutely did not. I've always suspected that that meeting was a test of whether I was trying something shady with weapons systems. Fortunately, I put a quick end to that. When I passed along Gulia's question about the U.S. buying Soviet MIGS to the Joint Chiefs of Staff, I was careful not to put myself into the deal. I don't even know if the Joint Chiefs bought the Russian jet fighters.

We then walked down into Union Square and played twenty questions. Mark was sober and professional, a very marked difference from his usual familiar (often drunken) demeanor with me. On the park bench the essence of what he let out (always maintaining "plausible deniability") was that Leonid's trip to Russia had been in connection with the

BNL/Iraqgate scandal.  Money from the Atlanta branch of an Italian bank ("BNL") had been laundered somehow through the Vatican. Although originally characterized as agricultural loans, to buy U.S. farm exports, the money ended up in Russia buying arms for Iraq. And when Iraq defaulted on the loans to the Italian bank, the U.S. taxpayer ended up covering the loss, effectively buying arms for Saddam.

Israeli intelligence had not been very thrilled by the whole thought of American money buying Scud missiles for Iraq to shoot at Israel. The Israelis had assassinated Gerald Bull, a Canadian arms dealer in Brussels who had been helping Iraq.  And the clear suggestion from Mark was that they may have killed Leonid as an example.  Mark urged me to look at Leonid's travel records and compare them to George H. W. Bush's travel records when he was President. There was a suggestion that Leonid had communicated with, or tried to communicate, with Bush. Because he would not, could not just deliver the story straight and maintain his "plausible deniability," I was left with hints of some diplomat's slip of the tongue during Bush's trip that tipped someone off as to what was happening and that got Leonid killed.

Mark also noted that Kissinger's consulting firm had a contract with BNL. I later found that Bush was meeting with Gorbachev in Helsinki while Leonid was travelling in Europe, a few days before his car crash in France. So now it appeared I had four sources indicating Leonid was a likely murder victim. But instead of the KGB as the likely culprit, Mark's information made it look more like the Israelis or the arms dealers trying to block Leonid from blowing their deal.

Mark thought that the odd phone calls to my office might be coming from Israeli intelligence. He thought they might enjoy seeing it all come out to the embarrassment of the people in Washington who had implemented the scheme. To sort it all out he actually told me to "follow the money," the supposed famous words of "Deep Throat" to Woodward and Bernstein during Watergate.

The money, I later found, may have been Leonid's secret bank account in London. So far, I haven't been able to follow it at all. And that's really a job for a government investigative committee. But after his death his kids found an account there to which $20,000 had been deposited and never mentioned to Leonid's tax accountant.

Finally, Mark added that Jackie had a three-person secret service detail, despite the usual rules that would deny her protection after so many years away from the White House. The recent Oliver Stone movie, "JFK," had resulted in a decision to restore the agents, given the uniqueness of the situation. Because of the movie suggesting that the CIA had been behind the JFK assassination, all kinds of crazies had come out of the woodwork to menace her. I had the distinct feeling Mark was dropping this detail about the Secret Service to give me a way to verify with Jackie that the other information was coming from authentic and well-informed sources. I never brought it up directly to her, but I did tell Paula about the conversation. Given Paula's comment that I should assume Jackie's apartment was bugged, it seemed to make perfect sense. (After Jackie's death Paula claimed that she had no real facts on which to base her comment about bugging, that she simply had supposed at one point it might have been going on.)

I faxed Paula a detailed summary of the San Francisco meeting.


**Chapter 21**

## At Jackie's Penthouse, Bugged Or Not

As I stepped off the private elevator into the penthouse the afternoon of June 23, 1992, Jackie was lovely (of course) in an olive silk suit of vertical stripes, alternately shiny and dull. I must confess I thought her shoes were goofy. They looked to me like clear plastic interspersed with tan leather. Oh well, what kind of fashion judge am I? But I do like jewelry, and especially emeralds, so I noticed she was wearing two rings. One was a simple gold band. The other was a delicate gold rope design with small emeralds all the way around. It was some of the prettiest emerald jewelry I have ever seen, but certainly not the most expensive. As with everything about her, there was good taste, artistry and quality without any excess. (One biography of her, *Jackie After Jack,"* appeared to describe the emerald ring and said JFK gave it to her after their newborn son, Patrick, died in 1962.)

The entryway had a nice small sculpture, maybe Greek, but I couldn't focus on it without being impolite. She led me to her library where I felt as if I had entered the absolute inner sanctum. It was about twelve feet by twelve feet, comfortable without being grand. There was a comfy brown cut-velvet or velour sofa showing some wear. It looked to be just the right place to put up your feet and read a good book. An oversized coffee table was covered with books, and books were stacked up under it covering the entire space. The big chair I chose was embracing and cozy, again a perfect place to sink in and read. Her personal writing desk was across the room, covered with photos of family (but of neither husband) with the biggest photo being her father. (JFK had signed the nuclear non-proliferation treaty on that desk. It sold for over $1.4 million in her estate auction.)

The mirror over the mantle had postcards and pictures of the grandkids stuck on it with scotch tape, and horses were apparent everywhere. The big painting over the sofa was horses.

The white-jacketed butler, served iced tea and finger sandwiches of salmon or cucumber. (I wondered if he had a black belt to go with the white jacket! It was this butler of whom Jerome reminded me in 2006 at the Hotel du Cap-Eden-Roc in Antibes.) The butler's arrival gave me my only chance to glance around. For again, Jackie made constant eye contact, and it was too delicious to relinquish even for a second.

An interesting detail that remains unclear: Jackie's long-time butler, Efigenio Pinheiro, is not necessarily the butler who served us and who I thought she addressed as "Francisco." Despite the similarities of the names, "Francisco" in my memory isn't a good match for Efigenio. I remember him as younger and taller than Efigenio. Given that Paula had said the butler had a black-belt and an intelligence source had told me that Jackie had again a Secret Service detail, it's possible that the "butler" was there to assure security as we talked about espionage and murder. Maybe in my second edition of this book I'll have that mystery answered.

Paula arrived and we all dove into the transcripts of my interview with Gulia in Leningrad. Jackie was unaware that Paula and I had edited out one commentary from Gulia about the relationship between Jackie and Leonid. Gulia had volunteered in the interviews that

*"I heard a number of presentations in the Voice of America with the stories about the Russian arms, etc., etc., about the pistol that belonged to Nikolai the First and then I learned that he worked together with Jackie Kennedy on the Russian costume book and I understood that it wouldn't be Leonid if he doesn't meet Jacqueline Kennedy, Jackie Onassis, because she's charming girl and Cardinal Slipyj* (Slipyj was Tarassuk's cellmate

in Siberia, head of the Ukrainian Catholic Church) *and Jackie Onassis just the same kind of people and definitely feel that yes, he should meet her somehow. So it was not surprising for me that they issued the book. The only one thing what surprised me was that it was only costume because he was never very strong about the costumes, but it didn't matter very much. I understood that they're very nice couple and they suit each other in many respects. I didn't know Jacqueline, but how she looked like. I understand that they could work in very good relations and I was very happy that they definitely work together."*

Paula thought it more discrete to omit the passage and that Jackie might be uncomfortable about the passage since it clearly implied a romantic liaison. And Gulia knew his old friend Leonid to be quite the lothario.

I had made an index of where we could find the key subjects, and Jackie zeroed in on the last entry – the French girlfriend. She wanted to see photos of her that Gulia had given me and asked what I knew about her and what Gulia had said. Later over coffee alone with me Paula indicated that Jackie had been very restrained in my presence in speaking of Leonid. Paula said Jackie had gushed about how good-looking Leonid had been and how attractive to women he was. It was the second time Paula had mentioned Jackie carrying on thus about Leonid's charms.

I recounted my experience in making the tapes and we all agreed that much more research was needed. I would file a Freedom of Information Request with the CIA to try to get Leonid's file, and also pursue the old girlfriend. (Years later when I got the CIA response to the Freedom of Information request page after page was virtually totally blacked out on national security grounds). We discussed whether it would be possible to get into the Vatican's files on Cardinal Slipyj, but we all doubted it, especially if it could embarrass the church. Jackie added that even Presidents of the U.S. don't know half of what's going on in their own administration.

Jackie was very concerned about Leonid's children and what effect it could have upon them to suddenly have fame and attention thrust upon them. She told me that she had received a letter from Leonid's daughter asking about my trustworthiness. Later the daughter gave me a copy of the answer Jackie wrote back in which she said:

*"...I can imagine how unnerving it must have been for you to have Philip Myers suddenly and unexpectedly enter your life. I have met with him twice and, yes, I do think you can trust him. He most definitely does have you and your brother's interests at heart... I told him that my loyalty was to your father whom I admired so much and who had been so wonderful to me, and that I thought he should proceed with caution...I think you should feel that Philip Myers and the people he has sought out – me and Paula – think your father was a noble man, and if they can do anything for him, it is certainly to not cause his children anxiety."*

She alluded to her own children coping with the spotlight and said that it was not such a big thing now because so much was known about their father. Her casual references to her children's father and to "Jack" gave me some license, I thought, to later send her some materials about JFK's connection with Cardinal Slipyj. At least a minor reference, and story-related seemed within bounds, notwithstanding Paula's admonition that one did not bring up the President to Jackie.

Jackie voiced her concern about the dangers of the spotlight for Leonid's children. Until now they had lived in anonymity. I added that even my student assistant's small experience of getting caught up in the intrigue had initially thrown him for a big loop, so I understood her concern.

We agreed that Leonid's children should participate in any profits that came from our project, and I felt that it was clearly a condition of her participation. It was her way of "helping Leonid."

I told them in more detail about Mark the Navy Seal's excited phone call, and then about the new anonymous call with the Gregorian chants. Both Jackie and Paula's jaws dropped, and they were absolutely amazed. Jackie was clearly delighted with the whole effort and was enjoying robustly the adventure of it all.

Jackie and I threw off a few comments in French for fun before I left. On the way out she mentioned that she was heading for Sweden the following week. Her son had gone kayaking there and in Finland and recommended it. Since I think she said she had never been there before, it would be a thrill. She seemed especially interested in the architecture.

Paula and I retired to the outdoor cafe at the five-star Stanhope Hotel. A few blocks down Fifth Avenue and across from the Metropolitan Museum, it seemed like the perfect place to debrief. I ran through various possible interpretations of all the bizarre events, including that it was all an exercise by the CIA to discredit Larry Wilson somehow. I was emphatic that I wanted to stay as far away from him as possible.

From New York I skipped down to Washington for some business meetings. I decided to pop in on an old college pal of mine, Doyle McManus, at the *Los Angeles Times* bureau. He was bureau chief. I happened to catch him just as he was going to walk over to the White House for a press conference. After giving him a quick summary on the way of my business ventures in Russia and doing a capsulized mutual catchup since college days, I told him there was something else about which I could not say much yet. He was quite surprised to learn that I had just met with Jackie and wanted to know what she was really like. I didn't tell him what the meeting was about, but just that there was something pretty explosive. If anything happened to me he would receive my research material from two different sources, and I wanted him to know it was legitimate. Doyle disappeared through the White House gates and I jumped in a cab. I felt a little safer knowing that anyone wanting to suppress any of the information I had uncovered couldn't do so by knocking me off, and I talked openly about that fact on the phone.


## Chapter 22

### *"Like A Cosmonaut"*

The reader must always remember that chasing old spy stories and the research with Jackie was a sideshow to the main event. Gulia and I were always looking for opportunities to launch high-tech ventures using the fruits of Soviet science.

"Launch" became the operative term once the Russian Space Agency got involved. Among the high-tech ventures that popped up on the radar was one involving Mercury 7 astronaut Gordon Cooper.  The Russian Space Agency and some folks in the Aero and Astro department at Stanford University wanted to test a theory for detecting earthquakes in advance from outer space.  The idea was that ahead of a quake a shift in the earth's magnetic field would occur. But it could be detected only from space.  Gordon Cooper was very much interested in this notion.  The instrument package that could do the job had to piggyback onto some missile launch already planned in order to keep the costs reasonable. And only one satellite launch in the foreseeable future would be suitable (these things are planned far in advance). It was a launch of a Russian spy satellite.

Of course, it would not be a good idea to upset the U.S. government that somehow my project was de facto financing a Russian spy satellite. All I didn't need was to get on the wrong side of the folks at CIA headquarters in Langley.

Thanks to the prestige of Cooper and Stanford there were some back-channel quiet discussions and the project was informally given a green light from Washington. Gulia's time at the Stanford Center for International Security and Arms Control had opened all the right doors. Through Dave Bernstein there (right hand man to Bill Perry, Clinton's first Secretary of Defense) we were able to float the idea to key people in the Pentagon and Langley.

Remarkably, Washington didn't blink. The fact that they de facto would be helping finance the launch of a spy satellite was AOK in the strange new world of cooperation.

With no objections raised, off I went with Gordon and Gulia to meet the Russian Space Agency in St. Petersburg. Fifteen years later, as facts began to tumble out about back-channel cooperation between certain elements in the old USSR and the USA, this OK for Washington to help finance the launch of a Russian spy satellite seemed less remarkable. But at the time, I was dumbfounded.

America's Mercury 7 astronauts were like gods in Russia. Those original space travelers were of mythic importance to the Russians. So, traveling there twice with Gordon Cooper, one of the seven, was quite an extraordinary experience for me. "Gordo" had always had the reputation of being the skirt-chaser bad boy of the Mercury 7. He used to get in trouble at NASA which wanted its "boys" to have a squeaky-clean all-American image, à la John Glenn.  But Gordo was naughty.

And he still was. Well into his 70's he certainly was keenly noting every buxom lady we came across during two trips.  Once when I asked Gordo about whether he'd ever gotten to know JFK, he told me one of my favorite stories ever.  He recounted that he was having dinner at the White House one night after having gotten in hot water with NASA for some kind of skirt-chasing indiscretion.  During dinner JFK elbowed him and said, "Gordon, I hear you're in trouble again." Cooper said he was mortified to have his Commander-in-Chief know of his bad behavior, but it was quickly relieved when JFK added, "We get in trouble a lot for the same thing don't we."

I had met Gordo because he had a business project with two old pals, one of whom happened to live up the street from me in Santa Barbara. My neighbor, Chuck Graffy, had been a test pilot at Edwards Air Force Base in the early 50's. The other fellow, Bill Statler, had been the prime designer of the SR70 Blackbird spy plane at the Lockheed Skunkworks, as well as the L1011 wide body passenger jet. Gordon, it turned out, had had a role in designing the U2 spy plane.

And now the three amigos wanted to build a new small twin-engine cargo jet for FedEx and freight haulers. They thought it would be a great idea to buy titanium aircraft parts from the former Soviet Union. Gordon wanted to travel to an air show in Moscow and check out the possibilities, using my connections to help open contacts with the old Soviet parts suppliers.

Gordon was welcomed with open arms in St. Petersburg. He was given the ultimate VIP guest suite in the City's official hotel across from the regional government HQ. There was an odd interpretation of a solarium, though to be fair, the Russians don't see as much sun as we do in California and relate to it oddly. And there was a huge living room complete with a piano and a large bedroom of course.

The Russians asked if Gordon would like to do a press conference, and the solarium seemed like the perfect place. Gulia alerted me that some of the questioners might be more akin to those from KGB debriefers than from news reporters, and he suggested I might give Gordon a heads-up not to treat them quite like average U.S. press. Gulia thought they were particularly interested in anything Gordon had to say about UFO's.

Geez, I thought. All I don't need is to get dragged into nuttiness about UFO's.

So I headed to the suite an hour early to spend a little time and warn Gordon. Imagine my utter and complete shock when he informed me that indeed he had seen UFO's when flying as an Air Force pilot. Furthermore, he said that when he was supervising some flight testing at Edwards in the early 1950's there had been a wildly odd experience. A filming crew ran into his office saying they had filmed a UFO land near them, extending legs, setting down, then taking off again when they approached. Gordon claimed he called the commanding general at Edwards to report the incident who told him not to look at the film and simply to prepare it for a courier to DC. Gordon being Gordon, he was naughty and looked at the film and said it showed exactly what the boys had claimed. And indeed, a courier arrived to take it away to oblivion. When I asked whatever happened to it, he was evasive at first. But then he gave a veiled suggestion that the best way to hide it would be not to classify it and keep it at the Air Force or CIA HQ. He thought it was more likely to be unclassified sitting in a drawer at a Coast Guard facility. I was fairly sure he knew what he was talking about.

Gordon went on and on and on and I understood more why the Russians might want to be able to ask him about what he knew. He said he was aware of one alien being living in Los Angeles and had met him. OK, now things had gone totally over the top. Here I was in the middle of the Russians debriefing a legendary member of the U.S. space program on its contact with aliens. And there was no swimming pool (infinity or otherwise) for me to use on that trip. Rather than getting grounded in the pool I was launching into orbital loonyness. In the "press conference" he was quite obliging answering everything presented to him. But they didn't ask the most outrageous questions about aliens among us, thank God.

In the formal meeting with the Russian Space Agency about the earthquake detection project, Gordon stopped the meeting cold and caused a minor crisis. He announced he was on the Board of Directors of a group that was building an air and space museum in Las Vegas. He wanted to buy one of Russia's space shuttles (copycats of the American shuttle) for the museum. If Gordon had one he could pilot it into Vegas himself if the Russians would launch it, rather than have it barged across the Atlantic. The Buran shuttle only flew a couple times (one of which was never acknowledged). He thought it would make a great display!

The Russian space agency seemed a bit taken back when he simply asked them for one. It wasn't exactly on our agenda for earthquake detection. After Gordon pitched them on selling a shuttle and said he wanted to launch it sub-orbitally so he could fly it into Vegas, he turned to me and asked if I wanted to go along for the ride!!! Good grief, I was about to be a cosmonaut (or would it be an astronaut??). At least I knew my heart was strong enough for it, courtesy of the Russian Academy of Sciences EKG machine. I smiled and said, "Sure Gordon, let's go!" Gulia intervened to get the meeting back on track and the question of my space travel was forgotten. But the Russian Space Agency folks seemed amused, and at least I got a great lapel pin of the Buran shuttle even though Gordon wasn't going to give me a lift home through space. For ultimately the shuttle wasn't for sale.

## Chapter 23

### *Woo Woo Voodoo*

Paula next decided she wanted to consult "Vladimir," her favorite Russian psychic and healer who lives in New York. She thought he might be able to give some clairvoyant insight into the details of Leonid's death. She said he could hold a photograph of the deceased and tell something or other. I agreed that she could borrow the photos of Leonid I left with Jackie, and Jackie was willing, even keen, to cooperate. Paula let me know Jackie had sent the photos over to her.

On July 10 Paula called me saying that during her session with Vladimir he had gotten extremely upset by the psychic energies unleashed. The experience had given him a bad headache, and Paula a stomach ache. She had shown him the clearest picture and asked about the manner of Leonid's demise. Vladimir felt it was definitely murder. He "saw" that the three weeks before Leonid's death was a period of great emotional stress with a sense of foreboding. He also "saw" two people unknown to Leonid who tried to get him to give up a brown case he was carrying.

He "felt" Leonid's enormous fear and thought the cause of death was a blow to the head. He also thought there was some involvement, whether as a perpetrator or a witness was unclear, of a woman with child of ten or twelve years. Paula faxed me a page of notes Vladimir made in Russian, and I asked my Russian friend, Leo, to translate.

Paula also said that Jackie had looked deep into Paula's eyes and said, **"Paula, I just love this project. What's new? What's happening? What did Vladimir say?"**

As an experiment, I decided to go through a similar exercise with a renowned psychic and trance channeller in Santa Barbara, Dr. Verna Yater. Verna was one of my small investors. Giving her absolutely no clues as to what Vladimir had said, I gave her the same photo Vladimir had worked from. She did the same routine of holding Leonid's photo between her palms. And to my amazement, she came up with virtually identical information, especially as it related to the sense of foreboding, a brown case, the death being a murder, and a woman witness.

I briefed Paula immediately. A few days later I spoke with her again, and she said she had discussed the two readings with Jackie who "expressed concern." Paula thought that the reality of the situation, i.e., of the possible murder, had hit home with Jackie more profoundly. Even though we had discussed the murder possibility before, for Jackie it really had sunk in with the readings from the two psychics.

On July 27 I wrote to Jackie, sending a copy of the article in the *New York Times* travel section that John Jr. wrote about his kayak trip to Finland and Sweden. In it he recounted a great threat to his group's safety from a storm that had popped up. Given Paula's comments about Jackie's concern over my safety, I thought I should say something. So, I turned around some of John's quotes about the dangers of kayaking in rough weather and applied them to my situation, writing to Jackie:

"I continue to watch our 'Leonid' venture very closely for signs that it isn't 'kayaking weather,' and I should hunker down a bit. So far, while it's occasionally breathtaking, I see no real signs of hazards. But I've never been more alert. As I have explained to Paula, when there's a trade-off between assuring safety and possibly risking the commercial value of the venture, I have no hesitation in opting for safety. A quick glance at my 4-year old's photo keeps me clear-headed... Since we seem to be treading into an area of potential current political sensitivity, the cross-currents can become extremely tricky. I easily imagine that my personal credibility may come under attack from some quarter."

Those words about my personal credibility coming under attack proved to be prophetic. In 2011 I underwent a brutal collapse of my business and my life as I explain later by sources anxious to discredit me.

And commenting on her new book, *The Last Tsar*, about the death of Tsar Nicholas II after the 1917 Bolshevik Revolution, I continued:

"Viscerally it affected me greatly, especially the latter portions with the explicit descriptions of the family's end. Perhaps because of my own adventure having begun at Tsarkoe Selo (note: it was the Czar's country residence), with the flavor of the Romanov household permeating the day when I learned of the treason by Leonid and Gulia, it all hit home. Gulia's comments about the KGB's potential reaction to the Leonid story (i.e., people would be liquidated by "accidents") simply served to make me feel that I had come closer to the Romanovs' reality than I ever expected. I was able to bring myself to finish the book, I think, when I realized that the message must be that over the long haul, it's virtually impossible to distort reality. And I'm biased to think that decency tends to prevail. Congratulations on publishing an important and excellent book. And thank you again for all your kind thoughts."

Again, I knew she would not miss the relevance of my comments to her own experience with Dallas and the mysteries that remained.

*The Last Tsar* includes graphic descriptions of the Tsar being gunned down in front of his wife before she was shot herself. I figured Jackie would know what I meant. She had sent me a copy of the book herself with a note saying, "I do hope you will find this book enthralling." I did.

## Chapter 24

### *Checking The Truth Of Leonid's Tale: Swordplay*

I had long wanted to find copies of the French fencing magazine, *L'Escrime Française*, to see what was written about the 1956 and 1957 demonstration fencing matches where Leonid had announced the plot to the French. And Leonid's daughter had invited me to come see Leonid's papers that she had kept. So, I carved out a weekend and headed for research purposes to D.C. and Atlanta.

The main reading room of the Library of Congress in D.C. is a grand circular space with a high dome. The antithesis of modern government blahness, the reading room abounds with warm woods and plush custom carpeting and ceiling frescoes. Anything less in such a grand architectural space would be blasphemous. It was a wonderful place to pour through musty old French periodicals, looking for pictures of conspirators swinging swords.

And I found them. Detailed articles in the magazine *L'Escrime Française* recounted the two French fencing matches in 1956 and 1957, with pictures of Leonid and the young girl virtually identical to those Gulia had given me. My confidence level that Gulia was feeding me reliable material soared. One magnificent photo shows the Russian fencers lined up on one side of a grand castle-like hall, the French on the other side, with their flags forming an arch between them. It looks like an Olympic closing ceremony, with flashbulbs popping and much pomp. I made copies of everything and shipped one set off to Jackie. The official publication of the French Fencing Federation noted that during the 1956 match "The microphone was handled by (Leonid), a conservator at the Hermitage Museum, who speaks an excellent French." It was heartening to see detail after detail of Gulia's story check out.

Bright and early the next morning, Sunday, I flew to Atlanta to meet Leonid's daughter. I had blocked out the entire day to go through Leonid's papers and bring his daughter, Irina, up to speed. Expecting a Manhattan sophisticate comfortably transplanted to the new Southern metropolis, I was surprised to find her a down-home, jeans-and-dogs kind of country girl living far out of town. At least she'd adapted perfectly after marrying a Georgia boy.  Full of spunk and perfectly ready to shoot any intruder in her woods with one of the many guns around the house, she seemed really grateful that I had taken the time to come fill her in personally about the bizarre history of her father.

Irina was in her mid-twenties, blond and not at all shy. She revealed a bit of a wild streak.  She had shocked her mother by posing for *Playboy*. She didn't seem to be exactly on the "mommy track." Given all I knew about Leonid's walk-on-the-wild-side audacity, I had to think that Irina was very much her father's daughter.  At one point, she wanted to talk alone with her husband for a few minutes so I took a stroll around the house. It seemed like some sort of little humor of the cosmos that her car's Georgia license plate started with the letters "PEM," my own initials. At that moment I had to think God was having a good chuckle with the whole thing. What on earth was I doing in the midst of a spy/murder/arms-dealing investigation with Jackie Kennedy? Any kind of reality check just left me laughing and shaking my head.

Irina, her husband and I (plus a couple imposing dogs) took a long walk through the dense woods to a nearby river as I recounted the bizarre events by which the story had unfolded. She showed me the letter Jackie had written to her vouching for my trustworthiness, so we didn't hold back at all with each other. Especially we focused on the possibility that her father had been murdered, and who the potential suspects were. She filled me in more about the fast and unsavory company that Larry Wilson, the arms dealer, kept.

His home sounded like a weapons depot from her description, with everything from automatic weapons to bazookas. And she recounted a tale of how, during one of her family's visits to Larry Wilson's estate, one of his millionaire Texan buddies had been present. Irina was uncertain how they were connected, but she told me that the Texan kept lots of files in his house about Leonid's battle to get an exit visa from the Soviet Union. That detail made me fairly certain that he had to have been involved with the committee Larry Wilson had organized to push for Leonid's departure from Leningrad. The Texan, she said, got drunk and crawled in bed with her one night. She had managed to push him away, but I found myself stuck with a strengthening image of a very unsavory bunch of people I never wanted to encounter.

She also recollected that her parents, before leaving for the fatal trip, had made a point of having wills drawn up. Since a trip to Europe had long been an annual event for them, she had thought it odd that this particular year they had made the effort to do the wills. She also remembered that just before the trip her mother commented darkly that she would never get to see her grandchildren. At the time, said Irina, she thought her mother was simply tired of waiting to see her children produce heirs. Given the new information, she thought perhaps her parents had sensed, or known, something was wrong. It meshed, at least, with the readings of the two psychics that Leonid had been alarmed for some weeks before his death.

Irina had files her father kept of slides of all his trips to Europe. He always talked about his European trips in great detail, she said, and loved to show his slides. But after the secret trip on the bogus passport to Russia, he had told the family essentially nothing about it. They knew he had gone, but totally out of character he didn't discuss it. The slide records also indicated that there may have been two secret trips to Russia in short order, one in late 1989 and another in January or February 1990. (Recall that Leonid died in September 1990).

Although his daughter had tossed out many of Leonid's things, there was a huge treasure trove remaining. Especially I was amazed at the loose-leaf notebooks with endless articles from the world press about Larry Wilson and the international committee he had headed up pressuring the Russians to give Leonid an exit visa in the early 70's. The articles said that he had first met Leonid in 1967 when visiting the Hermitage and had taken up his cause at that point. Irina recalled that the only westerners who ever visited her home in Leningrad were Larry Wilson and his associate from Helsinki, Heike Pohjoleinen.

Because of the wide assortment of American political figures who had signed on to support the committee's efforts, it certainly looked to me like Leonid had been a very important, even curiously important, focus of attention. It made sense, I thought, if he was really much more than a museum curator and American intelligence was paying back an old debt by trying to help get him out of the country. Again, it seemed at least to be totally consistent with Gulia's story.

Among Leonid's papers were also endless newspaper clippings about the major political figures involved in seeking his freedom from the Soviet Union as a leading Jewish dissident, including Senator Scoop Jackson. I also found (and informed Paula about) a record among Leonid's papers of a phone call he made in 1981 threatening to bomb the Soviet government's diplomatic installations in New York. At the time the Soviets were denying an exit visa to one of Soviet dissident, and legendary physicist, Andrei Sakharov's relatives. Leonid had called a government ministry in Moscow anonymously and threatened the bombing if they did not grant the exit visa. His daughter knew the story and confirmed it. She laughed riotously telling about the night her Dad's pal, an FBI agent, came to dinner and groused about the extra duty protecting the Soviet buildings from some mad bomber. Never, apparently, had he realized his friend Leonid was the "terrorist" in question. She also told how he used to stroll past the Soviet Mission's surveillance cameras trained on the sidewalk outside their New York building and flip them the bird.

His hostility to the Soviets was profound and unending. At one point when George H. W. Bush appeared to be too conciliatory towards Gorbachev and not insistent upon independence for Latvia, Lithuania and Estonia, Leonid mailed to Bush his Republican Party membership card with a blistering letter of criticism. Additionally, I had found among Leonid's papers a warm personal letter from former Treasury Secretary (during the Nixon administration) William T. ("Bill") Simon. As weird coincidences go, Simon had just bought a ranch near Santa Barbara from a friend of mine, an heiress to the Libby Glass fortune, and jauntily renamed it the "T-Bill Ranch," recalling his supervision of the U.S. government's issuance of treasury bills.

Most surprising was a letter from the late 70's from Jackie to Leonid telling him that she did not want to publish his life story since she didn't think it could be marketed to his satisfaction. Obviously, he had not bothered to tell her the juiciest details of the story at that time. Paula thought Jackie had no recollection of the old letter. I speculated at the time whether it meant Leonid had not come clean with the most important details of the warning plot, or whether Jackie, at the time, had been more cautious. Only much later did it occur to me that she didn't want his story told while he was alive and the both of them were engaged in covert activities. I'll never know the right interpretation, most likely.

Leonid's daughter mentioned that it seemed odd that although a British couple that had supposedly been killed in the same car crash with Leonid, where the police report (which she gave me) clearly blamed the crash on Leonid, no contact or claim ever came from the family of the Brits. It also seemed odd that they had been carrying a checkbook on a French bank.

I later hired a research assistant to visit the family's home in a working-class neighborhood of London. It appeared that they actually did exist and had died. At least that much of the auto crash story was legitimate. Whether or not they were innocent victims of a rigged auto accident I cannot say definitively. The French police report certainly makes it sound like an accident. But nobody checked, or had any reason to check, whether the car had been sabotaged or anything about the deaths falsified. The oddest thing about the police report was a notation that among the British man's personal effects was a watch with a logo of a Corvette club. The only

Corvette club we could find in London was a very elitist group, not the sort of thing a working-class couple in London was likely to be involved with.

After the Atlanta visit, I wanted to find Leonid's French fencer girlfriend. Gulia had said that he thought perhaps Leonid had confided in her the details of the plot. From *L'Escrime Française* I had the names of all the female fencers on the trip, only one of whom appeared to be French. A quick call to the French Fencing Federation in Paris produced the information that the lady fencer now lived in the city of Nîmes. I obtained her phone number and called one mightily surprised Madame Kate Delbarre D'Oriola. I thought she must be Leonid's inamorata, although Gulia was skeptical, not recalling the name. Now living in the south of France, Kate had just walked in the door from the Barcelona Olympics where she was helping with the French fencing team. Now she was married to a former French and World fencing champion who was also on that 1956 trip to Leningrad that launched the spy plot. She certainly vividly remembered Leonid and was willing to acknowledge that Leonid was "intelligent" and "cultivated" and that they were very compatible ("beaucoup sympathisés" was how she put it).

She professed total ignorance of any espionage. But then I was merely an alien voice out of nowhere, so I doubt she would have acknowledged anything if she did know it. Apart from the fact that the photos showed her to be quite lovely, her appeal was made obvious when she offered a story of her own sauciness. It was the sort of character, I thought, that would have appealed to Leonid. On the 1956 trip to Russia she had met the head of the Russian Fencing Federation, an official named Popov. She recalled refusing Popov's offer of a cigarette at their first Russian match in Moscow. She had fared poorly in Moscow but won later at the Leningrad matches. After the Leningrad matches he saw her smoking and expressed his surprise. She offered, "I smoke when I win! (Je fume quand je gagne!)." As a courtesy, I sent her a copy of some of the 1956 photos I had received from Gulia.

I also tracked down an Italian fencer who was on the 1956 trip, now living in Milan. He, too, had just returned from the Barcelona Olympics where he had visited with his old friend Kate, the French fencer. Eduardo confirmed that Leonid had visited him in Italy in Autumn 1989. This was just before Leonid's secret trip to Russia to buy arms for Saddam.

Confirming that Leonid was in Italy in late 1989, when Rick Ames, the KGB mole was posted to the CIA office in Rome (1986-1989), opened the likelihood that Ames had met with Leonid, or seen Leonid's CIA file revealing his treasonous past, before Leonid was cleared for the secret Russian trip. Ames had not been arrested yet, so the full importance of Leonid being in Italy just before the secret trip to Russia was not yet evident. But after Ames's arrest in 1993 the pieces fell together quickly. If Ames passed along the information to the KGB after Leonid's trip to Italy, it would explain why after all these years in the West the KGB had learned of Leonid's past and taken its revenge.

I wrote to Jackie to bring her up to speed on the conversations with the French and Italian fencers. I knew she'd be interested in what had transpired with Mme. Delbarre D'Oriola especially. I also threw in a copy of Cardinal Slipyj's "Thank You" note to JFK for helping to obtain his release from the Siberian prison camp where he had met Leonid. "How remarkable that of two cellmates in Siberia, one should enter your life and the other should owe his release partly to President Kennedy," I wrote to her. I added that the story of JFK's involvement in the Slipyj release is told in a book by Norman Cousins entitled *The Improbable Triumvirate*. It is the tale of the negotiations between JFK, the Pope, and Khrushchev that led to Slipyj's release.

Paula was shocked at my actions when I told her later about sending the JFK documents. She thought it explained a concerned comment Jackie had made to her about whether JFK somehow figured in the Leonid story. But clearly it didn't put a dent in Jackie's interest.

A few weeks later Jackie and Paula went to the theater together, and Paula told me Jackie had called ahead of their night out with a "girlish laugh" and asked for an update. Paula also mentioned that as they discussed the project and its hazards. Paula had expressed to Jackie her assumption that someone (CIA? FBI?) surely kept an eye open for any hazard to her and would alert her to it. Paula said Jackie expressed amazement at Paula's assumption and that it was absolutely wrong. She said nobody would do a thing to alert her to a problem. (I had always assumed that Jackie must have checked me out by some means to confirm that I wasn't a lunatic, but now I began to doubt it. Apparently, Jackie was going just on her own instincts in admitting me to her life and involving herself in such a dramatic story based on my information. She did as she pleased, and she trusted herself. My admiration for her rose again.)

Paula also said that Jackie had expressed some bafflement about some charity group that had tried to enlist her support since they had no obvious reason to be linked. She was wondering why they would bother with her other than the fact that she was well known. Paula retorted that she wasn't just well known, for heaven's sake, she was the most famous woman in the world, and by a lot. Jackie turned beet red with embarrassment, said Paula. I could easily imagine the scene, as Jackie was always the most unassuming and modest of people in all my contacts with her. Never was there even a hint of self-consciousness about being the legendary figure she was.

## Chapter 25

### *Jackie Meets Gulia: Back To The Penthouse*

In the fall of 1992, Gulia was finally due to come to New York as part of a high-level delegation organized by an Austrian bank, talking to possible investors in Russia. I alerted Jackie, and we settled on a meeting date, again at her apartment. To prepare for the meeting I gave Paula a long memo on the current status of the project assuming she'd brief Jackie as needed. It included the information that Gulia was aware that Leonid had made the secret trip to Russia, though all he knew about the purpose was that it was supposedly on behalf of a Finnish firm. Gulia had also confirmed that before the secret trip, Leonid had previously returned once to Russia on a tourist visa in his own name. So, it was perfectly reasonable for Leonid to travel there with Larry Wilson's friend, with no need for a false passport, if they were doing something innocuous. The fact that Leonid's daughter knew he used a fake passport on his second trip home, after a first trip under his true name, spoke volumes.

Gulia knew few details about it, except that Leonid told Gulia he had been well paid for the use of his expertise, and that they had met with someone at an artillery museum in Leningrad.

As noted before, after Leonid's death the children had discovered a bank account in London with approximately $20,000 in it, unknown to Leonid's tax accountant as well. I feel sure that the money was the payoff for the secret Russian trip (or trips). Leonid's cousin later claimed Leonid had likely received the money for editorial work on an Italian

Arms and Armaments publication. I can believe it came from Italy as part of the Iraqgate money laundering, but not for editorial work. Several sources confirmed that London was the center of the Iraqi arms procurement network, and the reader will recall that Mark, the Navy Seal/intelligence officer, had led me to believe the American money to buy Soviet arms was laundered through Rome. The Iraqgate arms deals were the subject of an HBO movie broadcast July 23, 1994, centered on the assassination of Gerald Bull, designer of a supergun for Saddam Hussein. He was shot dead in Brussels a couple days before Leonid's own death in France. Coincidences, coincidences, coincidences....

It is likely the KGB mole in the CIA, Rick Ames, was identified, or his identity confirmed, because of the attention we drew to Leonid's death. Ames supposedly was responsible for the deaths of several U.S. agents operating in Russia. But as the list of possible moles in the CIA was narrowed down, probably there was only one who could have been connected also with Leonid's death. That was Ames, the one who was at the CIA station in Rome and who had reason to see Leonid's file before Leonid made his secret trip to Russia in connection with the arms purchases for Iraq. Ames could have tipped off the KGB to Leonid's true past, about which they previously had been ignorant. A KGB revenge killing made sense and would have gone unnoticed but for the search for the mole and the accident of our focusing upon Leonid's death with a CIA Freedom of Information request (and my very tapped phone).

Before the meeting, I also told Paula and Jackie that Gulia was quite adamant that Leonid would never knowingly have done anything that even remotely benefitted the Soviet government. This included helping them earn money from the sale of arms. He thought that Leonid had possibly been exploited unknowingly in some way, and that Leonid had possibly tried to blow the whistle on the Metropolitan Museum guys or Larry Wilson buying Russian arms for Iraq with American money by contacting President Bush directly when he was in Helsinki. If Gulia was right and Leonid had tried to put a stop to the arms traffic between Russia and Iraq paid for with America money, it could have put Larry Wilson and his Finnish buddy in a very awkward position. Regardless of what they had told Leonid to get him to go to Russia, they almost certainly would not have wanted the arms traffic disrupted (and their commissions eliminated). On the other hand, Leonid was clearly beholden to Larry Wilson and his friends for their work on his behalf in obtaining his exit visa from Russia. And Gulia had known nothing about this whole aspect of Leonid's past until I informed him about it. So how much Leonid was clued in on whatever the real purpose was of the mystery trip is hard to judge.

But if Leonid had threatened their arms deal, it certainly gave a motive for Larry Wilson and his buddy in Helsinki to silence Leonid. For my own purposes, in defining future research and determining who I wanted to talk to, I had to consider them possible suspects in a murder. Leonid's cousin later gave me further reason to be concerned about Larry Wilson's role when he told me that Larry Wilson had pointedly refused to donate to the welfare fund for Leonid's children when Leonid died. It was odd, given the intimate relationship between Leonid and Larry Wilson that went back to 1967, and further suggested some sort of falling out at the end.

I listed several possible next steps for research, including trying to interview Nixon. Next I wrote to Jackie: "Nixon's role is particularly baffling in recent events. Haldeman has never gotten back to me, and I have not asked him why. My senses tell me that in three contacts to Nixon (two letters plus Haldeman), I've gotten absolutely zippo direct response and therefore I never will. On the other hand, after each such contact something notable has happened in terms of the story opening up or being confirmed through "intelligence sources." It may be a coincidence, a diversion to get me off on an unproductive tangent, or an intentional effort to feed me correct information. If I had to guess, I'd go for the last possibility as a hunch, especially since he had no control over Gulia and couldn't have known how much he knows or how much he would disclose to me. It would have been awfully risky to send me on a wild goose chase."

The prep work out of the way, I headed for New York. Gulia's schedule was tight, and he couldn't tell his associates why he needed some free time one late afternoon. Announcing that Jacqueline Kennedy Onassis wanted him to drop by her apartment would have generated entirely too many unwanted questions. I arranged a Lincoln Town Car to whisk Gulia from his business meeting in Rockefeller Center to Jackie's penthouse apartment.

Zipping through New York traffic in the unaccustomed splendor seemed to make him somewhat ill-at-ease. I hadn't appreciated the enormity for him of a meeting with the mythical Jackie. She and JFK had been the symbols of hope for an entire generation of Russians. Gulia maintains to this day that JFK's death was a greater blow for the Russian population than for the American, meaning for them an end to the signs of a thaw and an opening to the West that Khrushchev and JFK had begun after the Cuban Missile Crisis.

He chuckled in the chic little wooden elevator to see a sign taped up announcing that the hot water would be turned off at a future date to allow boiler repairs. The absence of hot water, sometimes for weeks, is a summer ritual in Russia as repairs are made to the cities' centralized steam heat systems. And it produces a summer ritual of griping about conditions in Russia. I'm sure it was the last thing he expected Jackie to have to endure.  It made his visit seem a little less like the ascent to Mt. Olympus. Nonetheless, in his own mind he truly was meeting a goddess.

Greeting us at the elevator, Jackie again was totally gracious.  We retired to the library and Jackie offered something to drink. Gulia knocked down a Scotch while Paula, Jackie and I sipped tea. Later he was afraid he'd made a faux pas in asking for hard liquor. I'd never seen him even slightly nervous in any situation, but clearly this one was affecting him a great deal.  Despite his nervousness at being in Jackie's presence, Gulia enthralled her for most of two hours with stories of Leonid and their little group. This time it was the two of them in constant eye contact, so for once, not riveted by her eyes, I was able to look around. If I had had any doubt about being in the inner sanctum, it was removed. There was a charming photo of a granddaughter on a pony, with birthday greetings to Grandma Jackie. The family photo albums, labeled "JOHN" or "CAROLINE" lined one wall. And behind me was her beautifully bound copy of *Profiles in Courage*, which President Kennedy had dedicated to her before it won the Pulitzer Prize as well as several books about the Kennedy Administration, including *A Thousand Days*.

Jackie seemed much moved by the courage of the small group and their motivation to stop the insanity of a nuclear first strike. She and Gulia connected in their warm admiration for Leonid, and the meeting seemed like two old friends remembering a third at his wake. Listening to the two of them, and taking in the scene, I had to think nobody would ever believe it if I put it in a movie. My truth was certainly better than any fiction I could conjure up.

After almost two hours she excused herself to attend to someone else who was arriving. We stretched our legs by walking over to the window for the view of Central Park. Her writing desk was arranged so that she could gaze out to the park as she sat there. I noticed no glamour photos of any sort, nothing of famous people or dazzling places. Everything seemed to be very personal and family-oriented, completely consistent with the modesty and unpretentiousness she exuded.

She returned and invited us to stay on as long as we liked to talk among ourselves, but Paula thought we should be on our way. She clearly did not want to impose upon Jackie's hospitality at all, even though Jackie's offer was quite genuine. Jackie saw us to the elevator, and for the first time referred to me as Philip instead of Mr. Myers as she told Gulia he could always be in touch with her through me. My heart leapt a little.

Paula, Gulia and I headed for the Stanhope Hotel, a couple blocks down Fifth Avenue, for dinner and a debriefing. The Stanhope lobby and restaurant are full of marble and fresh flowers. At first, I thought it would be nice to dine elegantly after such a grand occasion as Gulia's first meeting with Jackie. But as we sat there it seemed excessively contrived and just a bit over the top compared to the real elegance of Jackie's artistic simplicity. After dinner Gulia and I grabbed a cab to LaGuardia Airport. I had to fly him to Albany to catch up with the delegation, as they had more meetings early the next morning. The others had all spent the last few hours cooped up in a van driving to their next appointment, wondering why Gulia had broken off from the group and how he was possibly going to catch up to them. Late that night, when they arrived at their hotel, Gulia was mysteriously sitting in the lobby waiting for them, rested and relaxed. He never even tried to explain where he had been and how he got there ahead of them.

Before we had left Jackie's apartment Gulia asked Paula if she could arrange some small memento of the meeting. A few days later Gulia and I were mind-boggled to receive a collector's edition of *Profiles in Courage*, beautifully bound in leather just like her own, with her inscription: "For Gulia (she actually used his full name instead of the nickname), in memory of President Kennedy, with my best wishes and esteem. Jacqueline Kennedy."

She had instructed the Kennedy Library in Boston to send it to her specially and FedEx'd it to my office in California. Paula and I were both surprised that she used "Kennedy" instead of "Onassis," but she understood, I think, the enormous importance Gulia had attached to the meeting. He had explained a bit how she and the President were symbols to the whole Russian people of a possible better future. And he had poignantly told Paula and me how on a previous visit to Washington he had used his last dollars to buy flowers to place on JFK's grave. Gulia's reverence for JFK, Jackie, and all the hope they symbolized was obvious. I thought her sensitivity and kindness had again shone through in her choice of gift to him and her choice of words.

Gulia received the book from Jackie on the last day of his visit to Santa Barbara.

## Chapter 26

### *I Get Stealthy*

Gulia was a man of enormous resources and knowledge who seemed to have an infinite ability to know the inner workings of the Soviet Union and Russia. Perhaps I should have been beyond being astonished at anything Gulia would do, yet his next step left me gasping.

On one of my next trips to Russia we had gone to a meeting with some oil industry folks together with some chemical institute scientists to talk about oil spill cleanup technology. As we strolled along the street in Leningrad – a small group, about six people – Gulia slipped something in my jacket pocket. When I started to say something he just cut me off. Clearly, he didn't want to discuss it then and there. So only once I was alone again with him could I take a look. It was a chunk of material he described as being a sample of the Soviet stealth aircraft shielding material together with a formula for the coating material. Gulia explained that when he was a visitor at Stanford he had crossed swords with Bill Perry, widely credited with being the father of American stealth technology when he was in charge of R & D at the Pentagon. Perry had refused to believe Gulia that the Russians had the same technology. It was supposed to be a critical point of superiority for American warplanes. Gulia relished the idea of proving that Perry was wrong by having me deliver an actual sample of stealth material.

Again, I was in an "oh my God what now" moment. I had to decide whether to flush it down the toilet or carry it home. There wasn't much question in my mind that an export permit was out of the question. But once again, trusting that Gulia wouldn't lead me astray, I waltzed through customs at the airport and carried it home. Then I thought long and hard about what to do with it. In the meantime, I stashed the material in a safe deposit box at Home Savings a couple blocks from my office.

After a couple months, I confided in someone I knew who was in Naval Intelligence reserves. He made arrangements for an agent to retrieve the material. But I had him sign a receipt for it, noting that I had not asked for any compensation. The handoff was done in a bank lobby on my terms, under security cameras. The receipt and photos of the materials went into a safe place. I have photos of the material, a copy of the formula, and a receipt for it all from American intelligence.

## Chapter 27

### *Hitting The Wall: Spring 1994*

I heard about Jackie's cancer from the media, like most people. Non-Hodgkin's lymphoma is not necessarily the end game. She had a fighting chance, indeed, a very good chance at beating it. Or so the press said. Paula agreed, and said she'd been in touch and found her to be very upbeat despite being weak from the treatments.

At first Jackie kept working part-time. There were a few pictures of her strolling in Central Park with her friend Maurice Templesman. And I kept hoping that she'd bounce back and we would all soon be meeting again. Gulia was due in New York; ideally, we would all be able to reassemble.

But it was not to be.  Paula and Gulia and I went to dinner together and Paula agreed to get Gulia's greetings to Jackie.  He penned a charming note to her.   We still held out hope for a recovery, and even a couple of weeks before the end Paula gave me a fairly upbeat report.

I went ahead and sent Gulia's note and a new update to Jackie, together with a book in French, about the legendary female character "Carmen," of opera and literature.  It had just been published by a professor friend, Mary Collier at Westmont College in Santa Barbara.  I thought the professor's analysis of how Carmen became an enduring myth and a spiritual figure might strike some resonant chords.

Jackie received it May 14, 1994, five days before her death.  I thought Jackie would enjoy it greatly, particularly the complex and generally flattering analysis of the Carmen character as she appears in literature and music.  I quoted the conclusion (in French) to Jackie as I thought it would be meaningful to her, with the none-too-subtle suggestion between the lines that Jackie herself was a legendary and spiritual character.

It was simply crushing when she suddenly was gone a few days later, on May

19. I watched TV in some disbelief as her son informed the press that his mother has died at home, with her family around her. I could imagine them crowding into her private elevator that really would be jammed with four people, or clustered in the cheery yellow living room, as Jackie's life ebbed away. It was intensely personal for me. I had lost a great friend. And like a speeding car that suddenly hits a wall, I had seen an amazing life adventure, and a book project, crash brutally.

Still, nothing could prepare me for the next morning. I checked my mailbox, and trembled as I saw that distinctive blue stationary Jackie, and only Jackie, used. Truly a message from the dead; I had my last thank-you note from New York. It boggled my mind that on her deathbed she was aware of my research report and note to her and the Carmen book and had insisted on getting a note back to me.

Paula was insistent that we could not possibly publish anything as we still didn't have the whole story. We were of the same mind that there was more going on than merely a 1950's plot to warn of a nuclear first strike. And I had to agree. Suddenly I was very concerned with what had happened to the research reports I sent to Jackie at home. They clearly implicated various people at the

Metropolitan Museum in arms dealing, and conceivably much worse. And they also unequivocally could be read as connecting the dots between the JFK assassination and the Leonid murder.

Paula suggested I write to Nancy Tuckerman, Jackie's lifelong friend and assistant, and alert her to the issue. She said that Nancy would be helping oversee Jackie's archives, which were headed for storage for 50 years. So, it was unlikely anything I had sent would see the light of day. I laid out the problem in a letter addressed to Nancy and to John, Jr. and Caroline. The only response was a mass-mailed "Thank You" card from the children.

With that silent thud, I figured the book, code-named "Squished," was dead and buried with Jackie. I sat down, however, and from my recollections and eight hundred pages of research notes and documents, knocked out a quick draft sitting at the Santa Barbara Yacht Club with my laptop so that my recollections would be fresh. Then I went back to working exclusively on technology projects in Russia, and especially on software development and explosives detection technology.

After her death, I was further discouraged by the discovery of publication of disinformation about the heart of my adventures with her. The former director of the Metropolitan Museum of Art, Thomas Hoving, had published a book about his years there and in it a bizarre version of the relationship between Jackie and Leonid. In *Making the Mummies Dance*, published in 1993, the year before Jackie died, Hoving wrote about going to Russia with Jackie. She was there to do research for her first book, *In the Russian Style*, which was a catalog for an exhibit at the Metropolitan Museum of Art. Hoving writes that on that trip she had a secret agenda "to bring about the immigration of a member of the curatorial staff of the Hermitage, Leonid Tarassuk, a Jewish dissident and a member of the Arms and Armament Department. I paled, but Mrs. Onassis just smiled with supreme confidence. (Some years later Tarassuk did come to America and the Met, mostly thanks to her efforts)."

Unfortunately, this tale strongly contradicts the public record and Jackie's own statement that Tarassuk only became known to her via a call from Met employee Karl Katz, a supporter of Jewish causes. And there are *New York Times* articles about the committee headed by Senator Scoop Jackson that was openly and aggressively agitating for Tarassuk's exit visa. No secret agenda of Mrs.

Onassis was involved. Furthermore, Tarassuk was at the Met helping her prepare *In The Russian Style* which came out in 1976 and didn't arrive "some years later" as Hoving claimed.

So why would Hoving make such a bizarre assertion? I read it as intentional disinformation that would help the Met argue that its own people were not involved in the Tarassuk story and arms trading shenanigans. If they could shift the whole Tarassuk history to being her responsibility, it might give them deniability on other questions. But someone didn't do his homework or recall that the true story of Tarassuk's immigration had been printed widely in the newspapers.

The discovery of Hoving's book put a serious chill on my enthusiasm to press ahead with researching the unanswered questions. Plus, I was preoccupied with the business in Russia, my principal activity. And things there did not go terribly well even though Jackie had written to me expressing her best wishes that the Russian ventures would succeed. After getting a team of fifty-five programmers working for Fortune 500 companies such as Xerox, Honeywell, Chevron and Bank of America, Typhoon Software fizzled out with the general collapse of high tech in the late 90's. And the bomb detector effort went nowhere when the FAA refused to put money into Russian technology despite having initially indicated they would happily do so.  Russia was proving to be a dead-end street to match my dear friend's demise. Until September 11, 2001. The destruction of the World Trade Center started a whole new chapter in my Russian intrigues.

## Chapter 28

### *"Back In The USSR"*

After the attacks in New York on September 11, 2001, my phone rang off the hook. There was lots of interest again in any flavor of bomb detection equipment. The U.S. government hesitation about supporting Russian technology melted away as Putin signed on with Bush in the War on Terror. This change led me to chasing a fresh round of capital for Typhoon Security in Switzerland because of a Swiss contact in Santa Barbara.

The infinity pool at the Swissotel in Zurich is atop a 26-story building, in a glass cage. The smooth white tile edge blends into the skyline, so that it looks as if you can swim right out of the building into the sky. The edgeless pool is quite similar to the one at the Hotel du Cap-Eden-Roc that virtually blends with the sea.

In one of life's oddest coincidences I had booked a room there at the same time as the Dalai Lama. The luxurious marble-tiled lobby seemed to be a sea of Tibetan monks in flowing orange robes. Tibetan Monks were on their knees there doing a sand painting. The Starbucks in the lobby was constantly full of

Tibetan monks in flowing orange robes. I kept trying to contemplate a globalized world in which Tibetan monks are downing grande nonfat lattes in Switzerland.

I was there for money, not enlightenment, lattes or an infinity swim. I was there to meet Frederic Bezuidenhout.

If anyone had ever squished anyone in a trash can, I'd guess it was Frederic. Our common Swiss friend had introduced him as a South African intelligence agent (whether current or past was not quite clear and didn't seemingly matter). Tall, trim, ramrod straight in his 40's, he reminded me a great deal of Bob Haldeman, Nixon's White House Chief of Staff. My Swiss pal Fritz explained that he had seen letters from Vice-President Cheney and Secretary of Defense Rumsfeld to Frederic, and that he knew Frederic had been in the offices of heads of State (including, he claimed, President Putin!) and acted as a go-between for the U.S. with the Vatican at some point. The military bearing, the hint of intimidation, the utter self-assurance all suggested someone who can handle a dirty job.

The dirty job I had in mind was stopping terrorist bombings using various bomb detectors developed in Russia. Typhoon

Security Technology's mission was to build the machines in Holland and sell them worldwide, while supporting the ongoing Russian scientific work.

Ostensibly we met because Frederic had formed a Swiss foundation which wanted to invest half the necessary ten million dollars. And the other half was to come from a French/Swiss scientific foundation, the "Institut de la Vie" (Institut of Life, but we'll call it IDLV) to which Frederic was close.

Frederic's Swiss Attorney, a friend of Fritz Egger, Dr. Jean-Louis Von Planta, in Basel had even issued a letter advising Typhoon that the $10 million was expected momentarily and asking me where I wanted it delivered. I thought the deal was done! The Von Planta family was historically important and very rich. Jean-Louis's father had been Chairman of global pharmaceutical giant Novartis.

After a month went by since Dr. Von Planta's letter and no money had flowed into the Typhoon account, I headed to Zurich to meet Frederic and assess the situation. How could what appeared to be a nicely ordered situation in a nicely ordered country be seemingly so far off track? It was a major mystery, and I needed some answers fast.

In Swiss financial circles, it is simply NOT DONE for an attorney of Von Planta's standing to issue a "pre-advice" of $10 million and then have nothing happen. Something was disrupting the flow, and I needed badly to find out what and why. Of course, I was looking pretty stupid to my Russian associates who were expected now that Typhoon Security was ready to build a serious company around their technology.

Much of what Frederic explained about the IDLV began to echo what Gulia had told me about the efforts of that little group of Russians, including scientists, to warn the world if the Soviets were going to launch a first strike. Could it be, I wondered, that there was actually overlap between the Institut's Russian scientist friends and the brave few who were ready to warn the West of a nuclear first strike by the Communist party? Frederic claimed that the Institut knew Gulia very, very well.

The echoes became stronger and stronger over the five days. And then, just when I thought the whole Typhoon saga over the past 15 years could not get any stranger, Frederic announced that the Institut de la Vie was the Priory of Sion. I could hardly believe my ears. The quasi-mythical keepers of the secrets of early Christianity at the core of the

Da Vinci Code story were suddenly not only real but had signed on to be my new investors!? Good God, the Da Vinci Code perhaps was not just make-believe! Frederic claimed that its author, Dan Brown, had essentially gotten the story mostly right. Or maybe Frederic was out to destroy our entire venture by failing to come through with the funding intentionally. It was impossible to get a clear reading.

In no time flat Evert Blaauwendraad, a financier I was working with in the Netherlands, in whom I confided, did some research and found some very suggestive indications that there was a link between the Von Planta family and Pierre de Plantard (von Planta is more or less the German equivalent of the French "de Plantard"). Plantard claimed to be the most recent top honcho of the Priory of Sion and was interviewed by the BBC reporters who authored the 1982 English book *Holy Blood, Holy Grail*, one of the sources for the Da Vinci Code.

A swim in an infinity pool to the sky seemed like just the right thing!

## Chapter 29

### *Von Planta, Caesar and Dan Brown*

Who the heck were these people? If I had stumbled upon the Priory of Sion they were certainly not exactly behaving like masters of the universe. And why on earth would they reveal themselves to me?

Frederic spoke with near-reverence of a Frenchman, Benoit Boone, who was the de-facto head of the Institut de la Vie (IDLV). Over several days of meetings Frederic's story was essentially that at the end of World War II, before the Cold War got rolling, in 1945 there had been a meeting of key parties from the West (America, and Europe, but not the Orient, and including the Vatican). Those parties wanted to devise a scheme whereby Soviet Communists could be undermined using black ops financed by the money in the IDLV. Scientists across borders would be given access to technology and would share technology (notwithstanding political barriers) between Europe, Russia and the U.S. (Chinese and Arabs excluded). The result, he said, was creation of the *Institut de la Vie* which he claimed controls 43 percent of the deposits of Union Bank of Switzerland (UBS). And he claimed there were enormous funds elsewhere.

UBS was the world's largest bank, with something like two trillion dollars of assets under control. We were not talking chicken feed here. But it was also way too much to take at face value, an utterly fantastic claim.

Frederic claimed that at the end of World War II, in 1945, Switzerland (via its senior military commander, General Guisan) and the Catholic Church served as witnesses to the accord, and Switzerland was allocated drug and chemical industries, and finances as part of the rebuilding of the European economy. Louis Von Planta (lawyer Von Planta's father and former Chairman of drug company Novartis) was stated to have been a participant. The current President of the IDLV was the daughter of General Guisan, and she had also been President of the International Red Cross. There were bits and pieces of the story that I could verify, but much that was beyond any reality-check. To give me some ability to check the credibility of what he was saying he gave me an internet website address where I could find information about the IDLV (http://www.hsrd.ornl.gov/plants/index .html). It appeared to be a U.S. government site, the extensions to which indeed are all about the Institut. Prior to adding the extensions, it purported to be a site of the U.S. Nuclear Regulatory Commission (NRC) (http://www.hsrd.ornl.gov/). Once I'd pulled it up and seen that the link to the Nuclear Regulatory Commission was real, I thought I had really crossed some kind of barrier.

Frederic stated that the information on the IDLV website was classified and that when I checked it, the act would trigger automatic review of who was logging in. Having the IDLV information show up on a U.S. Nuclear Regulatory Commission website truly took my breath away. Whatever was going on here, the IDLV and Von Planta were not cranks, and somehow the U.S. NRC had embraced them.

There was also, on the NRC website, considerable information about a project about plant genetics. The emphasis on plants and genetics seemed highly suggestive of the whole Da Vinci code hypothesis about the bloodline of Christ and the symbolism of the vine for the bloodline. Plants/Von Planta/de Plantard: it was all beyond bizarre. Frederic claimed that the two key overseers of the IDLV funds) were an American Admiral, now about 83 years old, and Benoit B. Boone, a Frenchman. But there was also the clear suggestion that for the funds to be usable, the Americans had to acquiesce. And there was some problem between the Americans and the French over that issue. Frederic said that Boone's name appears on the documents of multiple central banks and he was at one point detained by the French police for two months because of the oddity of his name being on documents.  Frederic also said that Benoit's signature has been forged in recent years and IDLV's funds stolen, but that Benoit has a distinct genetic signature that cannot be faked since he has twenty-seven chromosomes (Frederic said genes but I'm sure he meant chromosomes) instead of the standard twenty-three. (I believe there are twenty-three doubles/pairs.) The first day in Zurich that I met with Frederic I told Russian stories of my fifteen years of travels there, including about taking Mercury 7 astronaut Gordon Cooper to Russia. I recounted how Gordon told me about an event at Edwards AFB in the early 1950's when a filming crew supposedly filmed a UFO. Cooper had told me he viewed the film and that it was as the crew described and was taken away in a pouch to D.C. at the order of the commanding general of Edwards. Gordon had also told me of seeing UFO's, and of knowing of an alien living in Los Angeles.

When I explained that I had met Cooper via Chuck Graffy who was a test pilot at Edwards in the early 1950's Frederic got very excited  He stated that Graffy was now the most important man in my life. He wanted me to call Graffy and ask if he could recall an admiral from that period and to drop the code name "Octavian." Frederic said that to do so would ring bells loudly and result certainly in

Octavian contacting me upon my return. A couple of days later, after I had had dinner with Benoit, he told me to call Graffy again and give him the name Benoit as the person interested in meeting the Admiral/Octavian. Frederic stated that the IDLV had had many operational problems since 1999 and had had money stolen from it repeatedly and that its connections in Russia had been greatly diminished needing now to be renewed. He said that Octavian and Benoit each had critical information that was necessary and that their meeting and mutual consent was required to restructure the finances and operations of IDLV.

He said that after my call to Graffy he had been contacted by someone in the U.S. claiming the Admiral was now insane, but that Frederic told the guy it was clearly not true and that "they" would know it if that were the case. I asked why, if they were well aware of Octavian's health status, they could not simply call him and ask for a meeting with Benoit. There was no sensible answer, other than it could not be done so directly. I asked who would replace Octavian as he is quite elderly. There was merely recognition that it was indeed an issue.

The IDLV was described as playing a role in coordinating development of scientific knowledge, at least some of which is derived from aliens. Frederic described "boxes" underground in Switzerland containing "plasma knowledge." He stated that the end of the Mayan calendar in 2012 did indeed point at a pending crisis with an approaching planet whose effects were potentially highly disruptive if not catastrophic for Earth. He said it was critical to get some scientific work moving; that the knowledge of how to handle it exists but it sounded like it needs to be applied. He also said that there are escape plans from Earth and escape vehicles and lists of who gets to go. The suggestion is that the exit point is in South America, and Benoit and Frederic had said they spent a lot of time and money in Brazil.

Frederic was as far over the edge as anyone I had encountered. I would have simply walked away. But I couldn't explain how a nutcase would have the U.S. Nuclear Regulatory Commission hosting his organization's website, nor how the billionaire Von Planta family would be cavorting with him. The source who introduced me to Von Planta, Fritz Egger, insisted that Von Planta was now a director of the J69 Foundation that Frederic had set up and which would be cooperating with the IDLV in investing in Typhoon Security.

Frederic claimed that Putin was selected to succeed Yeltsin by a committee of eight people, half Americans and half Russians. He also said Thursday night the 19th that he had spoken to the head of the FSB (new name for the KGB) about me and had confirmation of my profile as someone reliable and who makes things happen. However, he also said he was warned we could burn our fingers on the two companies we were dealing with in Russia regarding bomb detection technology. It was unclear, since Frederic was very intent on getting the Russian walk-through explosives detection portal built, especially for Italian and Papal security, how that meshed with him bad-mouthing the company that had developed it.

Frederic also had indicated that between Italy and the world soccer federation (FIFA) in Zurich, he was ready with orders for Typhoon for over 1500 walk-through bomb detector portals (i.e., sales of about $225 million) but was very nervous because he'd been asked directly by Italian security if IDLV was going forward with Typhoon's walk-through bomb detection portal. He said it would be a scandal if it didn't happen as Italian and Vatican security had passed on other products and built in purchasing plans for the Typhoon products. So, I emphasized that the delays in the funding were the risk factor, thus he needed to get the money to us pronto. Benoit was to come meet me with his "associate" and bodyguard (packing heat according to Fritz), Christophe Dosche. Frederic's preparation for the meeting had included a litany of details about Benoit that slid over into science fiction.

Benoit, he explained, was a human clone. Seeing as how I was unaware of any human clones walking the earth, I took this with a grain of salt, to put it mildly. At this point, all I could do was listen in wonderment. If Benoit was a clone then that technology was around in the mid-1960's, long before Dolly the sheep, the first cloned mammal, had hit the headlines. When Benoit finally appeared, he looked more like a standard paunchy chain-smoking middle-aged Frenchman. If he is the example of alien superior technology improving or saving the race, we are all in trouble.

Over drinks one evening at the Allegra hotel in suburban Zurich, Benoit and Christophe, Frederic, Fritz and I chatted in French for a couple hours about the need for the IDLV to reestablish ties to Russia that had atrophied. They claimed that until about 1991 (when the Soviet Union evaporated) there had been strong ties. Benoit insisted that Frederic turn over to me various books about the past proceedings and history of the Institut to bolster his claims. He thought they would help confirm to me the legitimacy of the IDLV.

Indeed, Frederic delivered about 3,000 pages of publications. Mostly they were very dry proceedings of scientific conferences and lists of participants during the 1970's and 1980's. The last sign of life in the IDLV, discernible from the books, was in 1991 when they put on a conference on AIDS. Conveniently, however, the books included the founding statutes and bylaws of the IDLV (from France) and of its supporting charitable foundation (from Switzerland). Finally, I had some real meat to work with and something I could use to try to connect the dots and find out what was real and what was baloney.

Being a lawyer, I dove right into analyzing them. Handily, there was a list of 1991 Directors. Benoit was not one of them. Indeed, I determined quickly that one of the 1991 directors listed there (and on the NRC-hosted website) was dead. Some months later Gulia confirmed he had known the fellow, a Dutch physicist, very well, giving some credibility to Frederic's claim that the IDLV knew about Gulia in detail.

Another 1991 IDLV director was Mme. Guisan, daughter of the Swiss commanding general in WW2, and a close family friend of

Von Planta's. Another was a Nobel-prize winning physicist at Brown University, Leon Cooper. With a little investigation, I found that Cooper was still reachable at Brown University.

The list of scientists who had participated in the IDLV's conferences was dazzling, and Cooper's presence on the Board (which showed both on the Nuclear Regulatory Commission website and in the documents Frederic gave me) seemed to lend serious credibility to the whole matter.

So not being shy, I picked up the phone and called Cooper at Brown University. He was astonished. He claimed that to his knowledge he was no longer a director and that the IDLV had no money. He said he had received a call from someone in the IDLV six months earlier from Paris to tell him it had all been dissolved.

Suddenly I had the possibility of major institutional fraud pretty solidly in front of me. According to the statutes, there was a well-established procedure for electing new directors. If Benoit and Guisan and Frederic and pals were in control of the IDLV they were apparently operating illegally. The IDLV statutes and bylaws they had given me made it clear that a prior director, Cooper, could not possibly have been kept in the dark about any transition to a new Board. The idea that they were improperly installed was further solidified by the fact that the website had not been updated despite my pointing out that it shows the 1991 directors instead of the current directors. If the current folks were properly installed they should have had authority to go into the site and update it.

I did a little quick Google research myself to see if I could identify Octavian. In Roman times, he was a great emperor, after the death of Julius Caesar, he took over and was Caesar Augustus (original name Octavian). It was he who defeated Marc Antony and Cleopatra and who ordered the census that caused Mary and Joseph's travel at the time of the birth of Christ. The quick top candidate was Stansfield Turner who graduated from Annapolis in 1946, where he was a classmate of Jimmy Carter (who studied nuclear technology). He got a degree afterwards at Oxford in Philosophy, Politics and Economics. Turner was later head of the War College and Carter named him CIA Director. He was retired then but still active at the University of Maryland. (I had the impression from something said during the meeting that Octavian was in the D.C. area still, so that seemed to fit.)

I tracked down a phone number and email for Stan Turner and simply called him, just as I had once done with Jackie. He indicated no knowledge of Octavian or the IDLV and said he wasn't interested in being in contact with them, although as with Leonid's old flame Kate the fencer, I was just a voice out of the wilderness. Nonetheless, Frederic's credibility hit a new low. He had said Octavian would be responsive. But I was more baffled than ever at why anyone would conjure up such stories and, most of all, take a week of his time with me to spin the tale. It just didn't add up.

Frederic had stated repeatedly that things he was telling me were highly classified. VERY ODD, as there was no admonition to me not to say anything about them to anyone. On the face of it it was a breach of his duty to be telling me such things. I told Frederic I wanted to see the original 1945 Protocol that the Swiss and the Church witnessed. Further I wanted to see the prioritization of scientific projects ASAP. I held back saying I wanted to meet the aliens. I never got to see the protocol or the list of scientific priorities. It well may all just be baloney or disinformation. But I'll be damned if I know why. And needless to say, I haven't been doing lunch with aliens (at least not that I know of!).

Later, Fritz Egger, the man who first introduced me to Frederic, said that the IDLV was in deep trouble, and Frederic had become virtually persona non-grata. There was an unequivocal statement that he had been working closely with Vice President Cheney and Secretary of Defense Rumsfeld whose correspondence Fritz claimed to have seen on Frederic's desk.

Fritz told me that the IDLV had failed to file the required charity tax reports with the Swiss government for the last three years, and that $800 million in their accounts had been frozen. Furthermore, it appeared that the current "directors" of the IDLV had absconded with $600 million of its other assets. And they had promised a million-dollar grant to a scholar at the University of Zurich, a friend of Von Planta's, but had never come up with the money. He said that he and Von Planta had been asked to join the IDLV board but that it was all under negotiation as Von Planta would require a massive cleanup of the IDLV's messy status.

I wrote a memo to Dr. Von Planta about all the institutional/legal problems of the IDLV and my conversations with Frederic. Fritz said the "new" directors feared Von Planta very much.

I insisted on meeting the other directors and off I went to Paris to meet the four French directors at the IDLV's offices at 45 Avenue Victor Hugo in the elegant 16th district of Paris, in sight of the Arc de Triomphe. The scene was right out of a 30's Hollywood film about Paris. Everything was antique, overstuffed, and expensive. They passed around ancient brandy that went down like velvet and puffed away on hideous French cigarettes designed to kill people off before they can collect their pensions, I think.

Louis Numisovichi, a wheezy, sickly old attorney, was supposedly the head of the Board. Others were Benoit Boone, Patrick Henriette, and Christophe Dosche (the bodyguard). (Note: Boone is very possibly not Benoit's real name; I saw one document that seemed to use another name for him but it wasn't clear and I was unable to get a copy.)

Fritz said that Louis was ill and had perhaps not a year to live, and that Patrick had no power. Benoit was supposedly the real power. But according to the legal documents, it was Louis as the top dog who had to initiate any move for special meetings or Board elections to clean up the organizational mess they were in. Fritz said that Von Planta and Mme. Guisan were dear old friends, Jean-Louis

Von Planta having played in her yard as a child.

I decided to stay as far away from the IDLV people as possible, and especially from Frederic. Whatever crazy maneuvers were going on there over control of whatever funds, it was not going to be helpful to me. If the IDLV is the Priory of Sion they don't seem like they could save themselves let alone the world. At one point, there was a clear statement that some of the U.S. "neocons" had dipped into the IDLV's funds for their own purposes, but no details were given.

But Von Planta is the real McCoy, a true aristocrat and power in Switzerland. One call from him and I was received like a long-lost best friend by the Head of Security of UBS. He proceeded to disclose major secrets about how the largest 65 banks evaluate and select security technology. I was astonished, and it certainly reinforced my opinion that Von Planta was a major power and not a flake at all. If Von Planta ends up as a director of the IDLV it is worth a fresh look. The fact that he was counsel to Frederic and a director of a foundation that Frederic established keeps me from dismissing the whole IDLV episode as the delusion of a bunch of crazies.

At the risk of overusing the phrase, just when thought things couldn't get any stranger, Paula told me she had worked with Dan Brown. She helped produce the collector's edition of *Angels and Demons*. How small could the world possibly be!


## Chapter 30

### *What Did Gulia Know and When Did He Know It?*

Gulia was a man of enormous resources and knowledge who seemed to have an infinite ability to know the inner workings of the Soviet Union and Russia. Through his friendship with the deceased Dutch Director of the IDLV, Prof. Casimir, I had connected him to that organization. I had an abiding problem, however, in understanding Gulia. I still, after all these years, could not understand exactly why he had told me the original story of Leonid and the band of brave Russians who wanted to save the world from nuclear holocaust.

He had challenged Bill Perry, father of stealth aircraft, in Perry's assumption that the Russians had nothing equivalent. I would love to know if Perry was convinced with Gulia's evidence that I carried back from Russia.

As Gulia and I progressed towards launch of the bomb detection venture using Russian technology, we found ourselves in Hawaii. Given the weirdness of the Swiss situation with, Frederic, Von Planta and Fritz, I had opened up an entirely different avenue for investment in Typhoon Security Technology. A group based in Hawaii had already put about $300,000 into the company, and they wanted us to come meet all their pals to talk about much bigger numbers.

An immediate reason for our meetings in Hawaii was to brief Hawaii Civil Defense and the U.S. Army authorities on the risks of a tsunami being generated by the offshore detonation of a hydrogen bomb. The idea had first been considered by the U.S. at the end of World War II as a way to soften up the beach defenses of Japan before an invasion. It had undergone an update in the 1960's taking into consideration the greater power of H-bombs. Amazingly the research papers were not classified and I was able to get copies, one from an author who had to dig it out of his garage. Gulia informed me that there was new research going on secretly between Russia and at least one of the U.S. National Labs (Los Alamos as I recall), using supercomputers to update the models and do risk assessments at various sites of a terrorist group or rogue country adopting the tactic.

The North Koreans, or Iran, or Al Qaeda could do horrendous damage, anonymously, and without ever getting a bomb near a port. As it turns out, a tramp steamer sunk sixty miles offshore Pearl Harbor with a hydrogen bomb onboard could send a tsunami thirty to a hundred feet high barreling into Pearl Harbor and Waikiki Beach at a hundred and twenty miles per hour.

Skyscrapers could topple over; Pearl Harbor be entirely wiped out. The symbolic value for an enemy would be gigantic. And the risk is very real. We met General Lee, head of Hawaiian Civil Defense, and with the army group in charge of disaster response for the entire Pacific. They would be required to clean up the mess from a Tsunami hitting Pearl Harbor and Honolulu, thus they had to understand the risk.

According to Gulia there were studies underway cooperatively between Los Alamos Labs in the U.S. and Russian labs on how to find a hydrogen bomb on a ship at sea. And there were even suggestions of how to find a facility in a village in the Pakistan or Afghan mountains where hydrogen bomb fuel was being produced using an oddball technique that took the process out of a big reactor and into a garage or hut. It involved burning mercury and would leave atmospheric traces that a drone could spot in the air.

Gulia continued to deliver the goods. He was taken very seriously at the highest levels in the U.S. security apparatus.

## Chapter 31

### *I Connect The Dots*

The quest to find large scale financing for the Russian tech ventures went on and on, often coming close to success but always with the huge headwind of institutional fear of political instability in Russia. I scaled back my efforts to untangle the story of Leonid's early-warning group of traitors. Yet, as the years went by and the bizarre coincidences piled up, I had to keep asking if there wasn't perhaps some unifying element to my adventures in Russia and with the Swiss and French of the IDLV. Since 1992 Paula had insisted that we couldn't write "the story" because we didn't know where it led, that it had to be part of something larger. I had agreed, but that left me really dead in the water until the IDLV frivolities started to connect the dots.

Year after year, in many quiet moments, I kept trying to figure out why Mrs. John Fitzgerald Kennedy Onassis had latched onto me and come along for the ride. I knew certain things that she wanted to have brought into the light. She wanted to know for sure if Leonid had been murdered. And I wanted to know what Jackie knew, and what gaps in her knowledge she had wanted to fill.

Jackie knew Gordon Cooper. Jackie knew Leonid. Jackie knew that every administration has its dirty little secrets, as she put it to me. I began to think Jackie knew or thought she knew who killed her husband, and who killed Leonid, another man that she had declared to me she loved.

In my mind, the big breakthrough came in 2004 when the *New York Times* intelligence writer, James Risen, and a 30-year CIA veteran, senior executive Milt Bearden, wrote a book about the 1980 denouement of the Cold War and the leading spy cases. In *The Main Enemy*, they reviewed Cold War spy stories from the 1980's, and they postulated that there had to be at least one more major Soviet mole in the U.S. government who had never been captured. They claimed that the Hanson case (KGB mole in the FBI) and Ames case (KGB mole in the CIA) couldn't explain all the deaths of betrayed agents.

Their conclusion that there had to be a "missing mole" was preceded by oddly placed discussion about the history of Bob Strauss, former Democratic National Chairman and Ambassador to Russia under the first President Bush. It made me sit bolt upright. Strauss, they said, started as a young FBI agent in Dallas in the 1940's, was close to J. Edgar Hoover, and then left the FBI to build a global powerhouse law firm representing high profile parties such as the Saudi Royal Family.

I began to wonder if their discussion of Strauss indicated they thought he could be the missing mole. One hypothesis formed in my mind that would tie all the pieces of *The Main Enemy* and my own saga together at last, including the weird anonymous call about the music in the 60's and 80's, the IDLV and back channel ties between "good" Soviet scientists and the West as opposed to "bad hardliner Soviets" and the equivalents in the US (e.g. J. Edgar Hoover).

The hypothesis that I thought was worth a look was that Strauss was the coordinator of the JFK assassination which was carried out by hard-line elements of the FBI (led by J. Edgar Hoover) cooperating with hardline elements from the USSR in order to stop the 1963 rapprochement between the USA and the USSR. If after the JFK assassination, the Soviets blackmailed Strauss, and he became the mole, the bits and pieces in my story together with those in *The Main Enemy* would fit together perfectly.

After the 1962 Cuban Missile Crisis JFK and Khrushchev had tried to begin a détente, an opening up of the two superpowers to each other. JFK outlined his ideas in a speech at American University in 1963. For hardliners in both countries such an idea was absolutely, positively unacceptable to the point of treasonous. Getting rid of both JFK and Krushchev, recast as peacemakers (or traitors depending on one's perspective) – gave common cause to mirror image hardliners in each country.

In this theory, it made perfect sense that Strauss was the music referred to in the notorious anonymous call to my office: "The music of the 60's is the same as the music in the late 80's." It certainly would fit well if Strauss were the "music", i.e., the link between the JFK and the Tarassuk assassinations, and was the missing Soviet mole described in *The Main Enemy*. And it made tons of sense thus for Strauss to have been sent to Moscow as Ambassador as the Soviet Union was failing, if one of the assignments he had was to watch for old secrets tumbling out that could embarrass the FBI, and maybe certain Texans. The first President Bush had sent Strauss to Moscow. It was the first time any hint of a Bush role in the events of the 60's or late 80's had popped up.

In 2016, I ran across someone who had been in the security community who agreed with my analysis and claimed that Strauss, on the day of the JFK assassination, was at the Hunt family compound in Dallas. The Hunts were reactionary oilmen closely aligned with Hoover.

And all of Gulia's convoluted efforts with me had established both the credibility and the means for the information to leak out via me.

I called the *New York Times* intelligence writer, James Risen, to discuss his appearance with his co-author on CSPAN to talk about their book and theory about the missing mole. I described my bona fides (including my familiarity with Doyle McManus of the *Los Angeles Times* whom he knows), and that I had worked with Mrs. Onassis on something related to their theory. I mentioned the Tarassuk case and a Freedom of Information Act request I sent in. He put me on hold and never came back. I called back and left my contact data on his voicemail and he never got back. It seemed extremely odd that he would drop the contact, however busy he was. I had to wonder if the *New York Times* writer has the story, and for some reason did not want to discuss it at that time.

Among the more staggering implications of this new hypothesis was that if Strauss, a high Democratic Party operative, were the mole, then the Watergate break-in at Democratic headquarters was possibly a legitimate national security operation as President Nixon had claimed. Up to now there has never been a good explanation for why the burglars were in the Watergate that night to bug it. On the surface it seemed like a pretty ridiculous thing for the Nixon White House to do. But if I am right, then Nixon couldn't explain it to the public, or perhaps even to the Democrats in Congress. It was possibly a question of national survival until the mole was found. Nothing could compromise that search.

This theory of Watergate, I thought, was wildly at odds with the version popularized by Washington Post reporter Bob Woodward, But when I read his own writings, especially his book about his secret information source, "Deep Throat", it  left me more certain I was on the right path as I'll explain later.

Gulia may have known the truth and wanted the mole exposed and the truth to come out by using me as a channel to

Haldeman and Jackie – the only way to tie it all together and make it credible. If the mole were found, and the mole had had a role in two murders of men Jackie loved, a lot of history would be reinterpreted.

It seemed increasingly likely that there was a "good" alliance between some Russians and Europeans and Americans (with a role originally of the Institut de la Vie/Priory of Sion) back in the 80's and early 90's who wanted to reduce tensions, to save the world, and a "bad" alliance of the hardliners on both sides that murdered JFK and Leonid and spied and lied and deposed Soviet Premier Krushchev shortly after the JFK assassination to stop détente. At least finally there was a framework for the conflicts and craziness of my twenty years living with this crazy tale. The chaos could be given some order. The dangers made more coherent and understandable. The strange waves appearing out of nowhere would make sense.

Those strange waves appearing from nowhere continued into 2009 and 2010. Jackie's old boss, Steve Rubin, at Doubleday commissioned a book by historian William Kuhn. A biography of Jackie focused on her last twenty years when she worked as a publisher, the Kuhn book took me by surprise. Kuhn called me out of the blue saying he had heard odd things about Tarassuk from Karl Katz (formerly of the Metropolitan Museum of Art in New York). Katz had recounted that Jackie thought Tarassuk perhaps had been murdered, and that there was an unfinished, unpublished manuscript about him with a Mr. Myers in California. Kuhn wanted to know more.

We spoke on and off over six months, and met once at the Athenaeum, a private library in Boston where he was writing his book. I shared some draft chapters of this book to help him understand my experience working with her on the book project. Notably I had scoffed at his suggestion that she seemed to be impulsive. Not at all, I responded. She was free, unconcerned about consequences that others might take into account in living their lives. But she was highly intentional. Paula completely agreed.

One day in 2010 Kuhn sent me a shocking email asking if Jackie had ever told me she worked for the CIA. He recounted that he had found correspondence from her to Vogue magazine in 1951 when she was right out of college, saying she might have to decline a prize from Vogue for an essay contest she had won. The problem, she said (according to Kuhn) was that she was considering taking a job with the CIA.

Apparently, this was before she had met JFK. Kuhn said he believed she had not taken the job, but the possibility cannot be dismissed. It would certainly explain a lot about why she was so intensely interested in what I knew about Tarassuk, other than a womanly curiosity about someone special to her. And the CIA has been known to arrange useful marriages, a process I have heard referred to as either "deep dipping" or "sheep dipping." A marriage of an impecunious but socially elevated young lady with a rich Senator with a possible stellar future might have been most advantageous to all parties in the early 1950's.

In 2010, I went to see Jackie's old boss, Steve Rubin, the publisher of Doubleday before he retired. He was startled by the possibility that the Metropolitan Museum had been used as an intelligence cover for the arms trade. He also had no recollection of Jackie approaching him about the Leonid story in 1992. That gap made me more seriously consider the possibility that she had intentionally misled me and taken the project out of Doubleday precisely because she needed to debrief me and keep control of what tumbled out. If she had taken that CIA job in 1951 and kept it, the "freelancing" of the story outside Doubleday made more sense. Her relationship with Leonid may well have been as an intelligence professional colleague. The possibility was starkly plausible and impossible to ignore. The remarkable speed with which she took me into her orbit and the way she moved the project away from Doubleday and put it entirely under her personal control fit well with that interpretation of her motives and role.

Just when I thought things could not get any stranger, someone in early 2010 who was conducting a security clearance background investigation for a newly-hired CIA agent dropped a bombshell. With no apparent connection to the background investigation of someone I didn't even know, he launched into a story with the new-hire claiming that the Watergate break-in had been a CIA job. The purpose was to look at why Cuban money had shown up in the Democratic National Party accounts. He said that the FBI had wanted nothing to do with the job.

I was stunned that someone directly linked to the CIA would put out such information in a way that was pretty well guaranteed to get recounted to me quickly. It was the first time I had any serious, credible information consistent with my theory that Bob Strauss could have been the mole and the Watergate break-in was related to finding evidence of it.

I found some a credible second source about the Cuban money.  In "Wedge: The Secret War Between the FBI and the CIA" (1994) author Mark Riebling writes that one of the Watergate burglars' bosses, on the White House staff, E. Howard Hunt (ex-CIA) said to another of the burglars' bosses, G. Gordon Liddy (both of whom were indicted for burglary) before the job that:

"There's a report that Castro's been getting money to the Democrats. The idea (of the burglary) is to photograph the list of contributors the Democrats are required to keep. Once we have those lists, we can have them checked to determine whether the contributors are bona fide or merely fronts for Castro or Hanoi money."

Then, incredibly, a couple weeks later I had occasion to have lunch in Georgetown with a former Political Director of the Democratic Party, attorney David Dunn, then at the Patton Boggs law firm. He told me he had been part of the team that moved into Democratic headquarters the day Jimmy Carter was inaugurated in 1977.  It was the last day Bob Strauss was DNC Chairman.  The incoming team was shocked to discover that there were no financial records of any kind: no bank statements, no checkbook, not even a lease on the offices. Everything had been sanitized.

While it is certainly nothing but circumstantial evidence, it is entirely consistent with the theory of Strauss as the "music" of the 60's and the late 80's, the common link. Perhaps there was a need to ditch financial records to avoid any risk of someone doing forensic accounting and finding shady Cuban funds at the DNC.

It is wildly unlikely that any smoking gun will fall out of the sky to prove (or disprove) my working hypothesis. And it would be a terrible injustice to an innocent man to accuse him of two murders and treason. Strauss passed away in 2014).   But as an obvious direction of further research, it is compelling. If the truth is otherwise, then it should show up.  The nature of the intelligence game is to obfuscate and build complexity. I am much too straightforward for it.  But eventually truth has a way of seeping out.  It is a wave in its own right, with greater power than individuals can hide in a wilderness of mirrors.  As I wrote to Jackie when she sent me her book *The Last Tsar* about the murders of Nicholas and Alexandra, truth cannot be suppressed forever.

Thanks to the development of social networking websites, the readers can help me unravel the truth and carry on with unraveling the curious story of Jacqueline Kennedy Onassis and Leonid Tarassuk, wherever it goes. The sequel to this book may just write itself!

## Chapter 32

### Betrayal, Arrest, Squished (Or Maybe Not!)

After Jackie's death in 1994 I did a quick draft of *SQUISHED* but then set the story aside. My focus remained the software outsourcing project in St. Petersburg, working with Gulia and our project in airport security technology (explosives detection). The software outsourcing venture, intended to show that Russia was a viable alternative to India, picked up customers from both Europe and the U.S. (Honeywell, Xerox, Telecom Italia, Novell, Chevron). It was the subject of an article in the Wall Street Journal Europe and also mentioned in a Forbes article on the Russian software industry.

I was invited twice to participate in seminars at Stanford on the software industry of Russia, sponsored by the Center International Security and Arms Control ("CISAC"). CISAC was headed by Bill Perry, the father of stealth technology when he was previously Undersecretary of Defense for Research and Development. Gulia knew him well from his time as a visiting professor at CISAC.

Alas, Typhoon Software fizzled out in the late 90's when an industry recession, the "tech wreck," caused a huge retrenchment among Typhoon's customers. They no longer wanted to invest in an experiment in opening a Russian operation. From a purely technical point of view Typhoon Software was a great success, showing that American companies could trust Russian engineers with critical work and coordinate everything on a daily basis though 5000 miles apart. The business plan had called for growing to 1000 programmers, with an average of 50 programmers for each of 20 customers. We had the first customer (Harris Corp., a defense contractor) at nearly the 50- programmer level, and several other Fortune 500's that had tried us and were happy. During the tech wreck slowdown, we didn't have any staying power, and once the tech industry recovered there was no more opportunity to find investment capital. As Putin became more hostile to the West it was hopeless to market Russian services to American companies.

Typhoon Security Technology Inc. (a California corporation), formed to commercialize bomb detection technology, had earlier partnered with Special Weapons Lab, Inc. (SWL) of Virginia to make a proposal to the Federal Aviation Administration, based on the FAA's informal guidance that they would chip in $2 million to bring the explosives detection technology to the U.S. for testing.

But the FAA ultimately refused and the project was in hibernation until after the 9/11 attacks. At that point interest in Washington perked up significantly. And Gulia introduced me to an even better project in Russia directed by a group of scientists out of the Ministry of Atomic Energy. The project had been classified before 9/11. We pitched the technology to the Office of Naval Research which showed interest. But they wanted the Russian scientists to fly to DC on their own nickel. After the bad experience of the FAA raising hopes then dashing them, the Russian scientists weren't about to believe the Navy if the Navy wasn't willing to commit some travel money. So the Russian scientists applied to a special NATO program closer to home in Brussels, Belgium, that promoted cooperation between NATO and Russia in limited areas, especially counterterrorism. Ultimately, they obtained millions in subsidies from NATO through a special NATO-Russia cooperation committee. (And US taxpayer money is the biggest source of NATO funding.) One of the two bomb detection machines was ready to leave the lab and go into production and was the subject of a NATO press release.

By late 2007 I had put together a $13 million financing package to start manufacturing of the Russia explosives detection equipment in Drachten, Holland. It included significant subsidies from the Dutch government, ongoing subsidies from NATO, and private equity of about $9 million. To get things moving faster, I found a lender in Alaska (a private family trust) to put up a bridge loan of $1 million. The money was primarily to be used to buy parts that took many months to get delivered. Alas, the world economic collapse in 2008 killed the Dutch financing and Typhoon Security came to a screeching halt, much to my distress as well as that of my investors. Typhoon Security was unable to repay the bridge loan on time in early 2008 and a downward spiral began. Nonetheless the product development work in the lab continued thanks to financing from NATO, and by 2014 the Russian technology for a walk-through portal had been successfully tested in a major European metro system and NATO announced the success of its "STANDEX" project.

After the Dutch financing package failed in 2008 I spent the next couple years casting about for replacement financing. Had I simply given up and filed bankruptcy for the corporation at that point, none of the disaster that was later to befall me would likely have happened. Businesses fail, sometimes, and in the aftermath of the 2008 recession investors were well-aware of it. But I felt a strong obligation to the investors to try to wait out the bad times and revive the company.  I didn't want to walk away from something that still had massive potential.  I had done a lot of strategic marketing, focused on the Middle East where the buyers (mostly intelligence services) were able to make quick decisions compared to the US. Over $50 million in orders were sitting there, waiting to be picked up as soon as I could give them delivery dates. And delivery dates required capital to get production running.  It was worth soldiering on.

In 2010, I was putting Humpty Dumpty back together again after finding support, I thought, from former U.S. intelligence community people working in a consulting group in D.C.  Jefferson Waterman International (JWI) and its affiliate, Fairmount Industries, in Dallas, agreed to help bring the Russian technology to the U.S. market. Initially they demanded 80% of the company for bringing in new financing and I agreed. Keeping 20% of something was better than 100% of nothing.  But their first effort to bring in the investment dollars failed and I forced a renegotiation. Under the new deal they could get about 20% of Typhoon Security. They wanted to move the California corporation to Nevada for various sensible reasons, including taxes.   Fairmount's "Cork" Jaeger then used his contact with the Dallas Ft. Worth airport, the University of Texas at Arlington and Siemens Corporation of Germany which was serious about becoming a global partner. I was excited, but behind the scenes things were coming to a disastrous head.

In Washington, as the Bill Kuhn biography of Jackie, *Reading Jackie,* was about to come out in 2010, I felt I should give the new investors/partners at Jefferson Waterman a heads-up about the chapter about me and my involvement with Gulia's spy story. It was my understanding that Charlie Waterman, President of JWI, had worked at the CIA many years and had played a key role in running the secret war against the Russians in Afghanistan in the 1980's (subject of the Tom Hanks movie "Charlie Wilson's War"). I was also told he had been CIA station chief in Saudi Arabia and had been the liaison who convinced the Saudis to bear half the cost of the war. Another member of the firm, I heard, had handled sensitive back-channel payments to a middle eastern potentate, delivering millions in cash each month in a suitcase at one point. I thought that cumulatively they had the pull to get the U.S. intelligence community to embrace the Russian technology and to help me attract investment dollars to replace what had evaporated in Holland in 2008.

Alas, when I told one of the JWI partners, Connaly Bedell (and old friend of the Clintons from Arkansas) about the whole situation somehow it tumbled out that "Cork" Jaeger's ex-father-in-law had been Bob Strauss, the main suspect in my mind for having been involved in coordinating the murders of Leonid and JFK and acting as a Soviet mole. Strauss's grandsons were Jaeger's sons, so the family honor was clearly at risk. I was aghast at finding that Strauss's familial connections had found their way into Typhoon Security and became very suspicious about how that might have happened.

I made the horrible mistake of telling Bedell about David Dunn's information about the peculiar lack of financial records at the Democratic National Committee headquarters when Strauss left and the reports of Cuban money in DNC accounts. I also said it was only the "tip of the iceberg." Bedell's loyalties certainly were more to Jaeger than to the new guy, me. Bedell walked away from the conversation with plenty of alarming information for his old buddy, Cork Jaeger, information that could be devastating for Bob Strauss and his family including the grandsons who were expected to come into Typhoon as executives.

The facts about the missing financial records when Strauss left as Chairman of the Democratic Party raised the possibility that the Watergate break-in had been a legitimate national security operation, looking for the missing Soviet mole in the form of the DNC's top fundraiser, Bob Strauss.

About the same time a disgruntled former business partner of mine, who was on a personal vendetta against me, discovered my relationship with JWI in DC and contacted them in an effort to attack me.   An alcoholic and crystal meth user, this former partner had never forgiven me for pointing out his apparent substance abuse. He had resisted all efforts to get him into rehab back in 2004. Instead he held a grudge, blamed me for his subsequent failures in business, and he set out to destroy me. He made false police reports that I was lying to people about the Russian technology even existing let alone my company's rights to use it. The former partner falsely claimed I had stolen and stashed $20 million overseas, and that I had never actually had rights to the Russian technology. Both claims were complete fabrications but they got the attention of prosecutors, and a handful of unhappy investors.

This ex-partner's own investors had sued him in a very, very nasty piece of litigation claiming that he has drunk up his company's money and fraudulently issued himself and an ally sixteen million shares of stock without getting Board or Shareholder approval. At the time he was selling that stock to outsiders for $5/share, so what he arrogated unto himself was worth potentially $80 million, and taxable. But he reported nothing to the IRS. Later the IRS debriefed me at length as it considered whether to hit him with huge tax penalties, and that surely made his resentment worse. The fight with his shareholders was a very bitter battle. When finally he settled it by giving up any claim to some stock in Typhoon Security Technology, he decided to do whatever he could to take down Typhoon and myself. He was not about to let his antagonistic investors profit from Typhoon Security's success since he had lost all his stock interests in Typhoon.

I was really horrified when the JWI people showed me an email from the ex-partner trying to disrupt our business.

About ten days after the conversation with Bedell and shortly after the ex-partner connected with JWI, I was arrested while on a business trip in Atlanta and charged with irregularities and deception in my business dealings. At first, I was baffled. Then I put two and two together. The ex-partner gave

Jaeger and JWI a path to get me out of the way, to try to take 100% ownership of the bomb detection company by shifting it into a new corporation Jaeger set up, and to destroy my credibility on the Strauss-as-Soviet-mole theory.

Then the Chief Financial Officer of Typhoon Security, a business associate in Atlanta, said that Jaeger had contacted him and instructed him to destroy some critical documents (evidence!) that were very favorable to me. The documents showed that my company had had the rights to the technology and that all my investors were going to share in the profits from the project. One of the ex-partner's lies to the prosecutors was that I had formed the Nevada corporation and moved the security technology business into it as a way to cut out the old investors. But the ex-partner's claims that I was stealing from and short-changing the investors was nonsense. I had formed the Nevada corporation with the old investors being even larger owners than before via a special trust. Jaeger wanted the trust documents destroyed that proved that I had protected the old investors, according to the fellow in Atlanta who recounted the call. Jaeger proceeded to form a new corporation and tried to steal my relationship with the Russian lab and with Siemens when I was helpless to do anything about it. I didn't have an investor list and business communications were virtually impossible from jail. I was also enormously traumatized and battling like crazy just to keep myself together and do what I could to fight the charges.

I was vulnerable, alas, because of one screw-up in my paperwork for raising money. My former office manager had failed to inform me of a letter from the State of California that an annual one-page statement identifying our corporate officers and directors was late. Of course, it was the office manager's job to see to that detail or at least to alert me to it. I was running around Holland trying to save the day. Nonetheless it was absolutely my fault that the office didn't run efficiently and that I didn't know about the lateness of the filing. As a result, Typhoon Security Technology had been suspended and when I took a million-dollar bridge loan in December 2007, the company didn't have the legal right to borrow that money.

That was the glitch that tripped me up.

I didn't know the company had been suspended and couldn't borrow, but it was certainly my responsibility to know it. I have only myself to blame for the slipup in the regulatory paperwork. But what should have been easily fixed and triggered a slap on the hand for a missed one-page annual statement, turned into, literally, a federal case because of all the claims of the ex-partner that were false. It was intensely frustrating, and certainly I'm very sorry to the investors who took losses. But by no means were the ex-partner's big lies true.

The big shocker was that I found out that the spy book project and the business interests had intersected. The new investor group in DC that I thought was to be its salvation included the former son-in-law of Bob Strauss, my candidate to be the missing Soviet mole. To put it mildly, he had an incentive to destroy my credibility and get me out of the picture.

While in jail battling my case, I read several books that jolted me and reinforced my notion that something very foul had happened to me. Everything reinforced my theory about Strauss being the missing Soviet mole, involved in two murders. And Jaeger's reaction to my situation, trying to have evidence destroyed, greatly reinforced my belief that I had it right.

To understand the impact of what I found, the reader needs to have a basic understanding of the Watergate scandal that led to President Nixon's resignation. Five burglars were caught inside the offices of the Democratic National Committee in the middle of the night, trying to bug the offices. The big question has always been why? Two of them had a White House official's phone number in his phone book, and the burglars all had intelligence backgrounds. The White House called it a "third-rate burglary" and proceeded to cover up its ties to the burglars. Nixon's people diverted campaign donations into cash payments for hush money to keep the burglars from talking. Eventually the truth tumbled out that Nixon had tried to use the CIA to block the criminal investigation on the grounds that it was a national security matter. His support in Congress collapsed and he resigned.

As much as I had learned, from David Dunn and the CIA background checker, even I was astonished as I kept finding more details to support the idea of Strauss as a Soviet mole. I read Watergate burglar G. Gordon Liddy's autobiography in which he notes that just prior to the Watergate break-in he had been tapping and recording Bob Strauss's car phone. He doesn't explain why, but says he so informed the Nixon White House. I also read *Veil* by Bob Woodward, one of the *Washington Post* journalists who drove the Watergate story and co-author of *All the President's Men*. His subsequent book, *Veil,* was about the CIA under Reagan and its various secretive initiatives. To my enormous surprise, Woodward wrote that JWI President Charlie Waterman (one of my new partners who was supposed to be helping me revive Typhoon Security), had been fired by the CIA after an FBI investigation concluded he had leaked classified information. Suddenly I was kicking myself for not having checked out the people at JWI more thoroughly before joining forces with them.

Furthermore Woodward's 2005 book *The Secret Man* tells the story of his secret information source during Watergate, Mark Felt, known as DEEP THROAT. Felt's job was Deputy Director of the FBI, but his identity had been kept secret for decades. To the world he was only known as: DEEP THROAT. Curiously, Woodward tells about Nixon, later, testifying on behalf of Felt when he was indicted for using illegal surveillance tactics on a terrorist group. Woodward tried to make sense of Nixon's cooperation benefitting his supposed betrayer, DEEP THROAT, stating:

*"I suspect the testimony was part of Nixon's effort to stage a comeback and show that his national security concerns (in Watergate) were valid."*

What if Nixon were right that the Watergate burglary really was a national security matter?  What if Woodward were right that Nixon was trying to win that point as part of his restoration to the status of foreign policy guru? I was feeling more and more confident about my hypothesis that had been reinforced by the story of Cuban money in the Democratic Party accounts.

Woodward recounts his surprise that Felt was an admirer of FBI Director J. Edgar Hoover.  Later he speculates on Felt's motives in serving as the anonymous source of Watergate information. But he never nails it down. He recounts that many years later when he visited Felt, who was suffering from dementia, he wanted to ask but could not, "Why were you Deep Throat? What was your motive? Who are you? Who were you?"

Woodward's book certainly is consistent with my theory that Strauss and Hoover were involved in the JFK and Leonid assassinations and Nixon, with the Watergate break-in, was on the trail of a genuine national security issue. It makes sense that he had his CIA-related White House people like Howard Hunt and James McCord try to bug Democratic Party headquarters at the Watergate complex instead of doing the legal, and orthodox, thing of having the FBI do the job.  Normally the FBI and only the FBI should be doing such a domestic surveillance job. But of course, Nixon couldn't use them if the FBI director, Hoover, himself, was under suspicion of having conspired with Bob Strauss, his close friend, to assassinate John Kennedy.

Woodward even goes so far as to write "Was it possible, I wondered, that somehow being Deep Throat and talking to me was Bureau policy, a final decision he had made."

If Deep Throat's leaking of information that brought Nixon down was FBI policy, and Deep Throat did not go rogue as was popularly believed, it fits perfectly with my theory. Felt, in effect, protected the FBI from revelations about Hoover and Strauss's roles in assassinating JFK. The antagonism between Hoover's FBI and the CIA is well known. See Riebling's "*Wedge, the Secret War Between the FBI and the CIA.*"

It struck me as entirely plausible that Deep Throat (Mark Felt), a profound admirer of J. Edgar Hoover, had as part of his motivation to talk to Woodward his agency's need to take down Nixon and keep the role of Strauss hidden so as to limit a threat to the FBI and Hoover's reputation. If uncovering Strauss was the key to Hoover's role in the assassination, a Hoover loyalist would have wanted to stop Nixon and the CIA's investigation of Strauss, including the Cuban money going into the Democratic National Committee accounts, and of the quest for Russian moles. It would be consistent with that scenario that the CIA or CIA-friendly parties could have been feeding me research clues like the anonymous "music" call, and the help of Jackie finding out just exactly what a good guy Russian Gulia knew about the truth. The CIA and FBI hostility could have been profoundly played out in the Tarassuk story and my research of it.

So despite my naïve belief that I could keep the Russian technology business and the spy book project with Jackie compartmentalized, they fully intersected. I had inadvertently ended up with business partners who, because of their links to Strauss and shady backgrounds, had every incentive to have me discredited and moved out of my position as Typhoon Security CEO. They were also aggrieved because they had originally demanded 80% of Typhoon Security in exchange for bringing in financing. When they didn't perform initially, I cut them back to about 20% as they continued efforts. They were not happy and when it seemed Siemens was about to sign on, they wanted to get rid of me and take 100% by pushing the project into a new corporation they formed.

I alerted Gulia to the Jaeger/Strauss link but otherwise could do nothing to determine the fate of Typhoon Security Technology or to salvage any part of it. The rest of the Typhoon management staff was like the proverbial deer frozen in the headlights. Without me driving the process, Typhoon Security collapsed.

Whether or not my hypothesis is correct about Bob Strauss being the "music" of the "60's and late 80's" that was involved with two murders and served his Russian blackmailers will someday perhaps be determined. Strauss died in March 2014.

**Chapter 33:** What was that all about?

When Jackie died, she, Paula and I were all of the opinion that the Leonid story was part of something much bigger. And the book shouldn't be published until the full story could be revealed. It took a long time for me to be satisfied that I had the essence right.

I got two replies from the CIA to Freedom of Information Act requests that reinforced the idea that something much bigger than just the 1950's early warning plot was in play.  About 2004 I received a reply to the Freedom of Information Act request I had sent seeking Leonid's file. Virtually everything was blacked out, with a cover sheet indicating that the CIA was invoking national security exceptions to the disclosure laws. In 2012, I got another CIA Freedom of Information Act response saying that absolutely nothing about our quest for information about Leonid, the mole hunt or Jackie's involvement could be released because it was all classified on national security grounds. So, we were definitely not chasing illusions.

In the end, I believe I identified what the whole Leonid story was part of: the mole hunt, the secret slush fund of the IDLV in Paris, and who was behind the murders of the two men in Jackie's life. She understood, I'm sure, from the early Angleton/Nosenko conversation and the later weird anonymous calls, that we were dealing potentially with such large issues. Hopefully publishing this story will help the rest of the truth tumble out.

The big question is whether Jackie was being straight with me, and whether her interests in Leonid were as she represented them. Or was she obscuring some Intelligence role of her own that tied into the Leonid history. There is ample evidence for both interpretations of her actions. Much more research might tip the balance definitively one way or the other. The lawyer in me wants to look at hard evidence and make a case beyond a reasonable doubt. But that is impossible. In my heart, however, I think Jackie was being straight with me. There was a lack of guile, a solidity and openness and kindness I experienced. I really don't think she was faking it. When she showed concern about my safety, I don't think she was doing so for any reason other than decency that went hand-in-hand with astute analysis. In my mind, the lady was smart, kind, decent and actually surprisingly uncomplex. She was free. She was beyond obfuscation. She was clear.

If Jackie were alive, oh what fun we would have finally writing the last chapter of *SQUISHED*.

Did I end up "squished in a trash can somewhere" as Jackie predicted in 1991? Was it because of what Gulia told me that day as we watched his son play on the swing set near Leningrad in 1991? I lost my business and became bankrupt and ended up in prison on largely trumped-up charges. (Prosecutors get excited when they think you've stashed $20 million somewhere!) But perhaps there's another chapter of my own life yet to be written. And hopefully happier music will play. And the truth will set me free.

I was released from prison February 6, 2017. My first order of business was to get *SQUISHED* into publication.

Thank you, Jackie, for all your help.

OTHER BOOKS BY PHILIP MYERS:
SEE: FACEBOOK.COM/PHILMYERS AUTHOR
OR  WWW.PHILMYERSAUTHOR.COM

## THE SLUSH FUND SERIES:

5 Historical fiction books built on the truth that at the end of WW2, The Vatican, Swiss, CIA, and MI6 shifted massive funds the Nazis had seized from the Jews to the predecessor of UBS, in Geneva, to create a source of support for black ops to subvert the Soviet Union. Add in the discovery by a young Stanford grad (Shane Cochran) that he is the ranking member of the bloodline of Christ and also a descendant of the Count of Flanders who is the historical source of the Holy Grail legend, and that the Muslim tradition is right: Christ survived the crucifixion. He went with his family to France, wrote "Q" which biblical scholars consider the source material for 3 of the gospels, and in which he explained "miracles" in terms of quantum physics and holography, specifying that it was only to be revealed when those ideas became established.

**SLUSH FUND 1: The Toxic Treasure**
Parallel stories in 2014 and 1944 as the Stanford grad discovers the history of creation of the Slush Fund, and the way it was created is detailed.

**SLUSH FUND 2: The Prince of Lorraine**
Parallel stories in 2011 and AD 33 as Cochran battles Nazi families in Brazil who are trying to recoup the funds, and Christ and his family flee to Alexandria and Marseilles.

**SLUSH FUND 3: Christ Uses the Internet at Last**

The fight over control of the Slush Fund rages with the Swiss branch of the bloodline. Cochran reveals the existence of "Q" in a webcast from the top of the dome of St. Peters.

**SLUSH FUND 4: The first Conscious machine**
Russian physicists use technology suggested in "Q" to build a device that controls wormholes and gives a massive military advantage. The device is sentient and must choose who to obey.

**SLUSH FUND 5:  Killer Dreaming**
The Russians chase Cochran who has the sentient machine that controls wormholes. His fate depends on a young lady writer who has shared his dream of death on the airport runway in Santa Barbara.

## THE REHAB SERIES (4 books)

4 books in which the lead characters Rick Johnson and Ellen Tognazzini, two type-A overachiever personalities marry  young, divorce and find each other again many years later. As true loves, now wealthy and powerful, they take on many global challenges. Rick always thinks outside the box. Ellen grounds him. Something of the flavor of the old Hart to Hart TV show. Great Fun reads!!

## CORPORATE REHAB:
Rick and Ellen, the golden couple, marry young and divorce fast. 30 years later, with Rick in jail in Santa Barbara, his corporate empire collapsed. He watches alcoholics and addicts go out to rehab and gets the idea to convince the private company (a nationwide organization) that runs the jail, to launch a white-collar rehab program at an old beachfront hotel in Santa Barbara, at luxury rates with room service. He becomes the first resident and befriends a young entrepreneur living next to the hotel on

Miramar Beach. He is trying to build a solar energy company but is out of his depth. Rick becomes the eminence grise and rapidly builds the company using Russian technology and sells it for a fortune. Rick's ex-wife, Ellen, is a county supervisor who is close to the jail management company. They reconnect and remarry.

## CONGRESSIONAL REHAB:
Ellen has been elected to Congress. Rick is taking it easy, when US goes into a financial crisis when China quits lending, disgusted with Congressional dysfunction. Rick conceives a solution, a Congressional continuing education program with a hidden feature: it requires all Congressmen to go to jail for a week to learn humility and get a grip on the need for solving problems. Congress passes it without understanding it; the public loves it. The book follows three Congressmen having the jail experience; a pro-NRA Conservative from Idaho who hates the idea, a Southern aristocratic democrat who likes the idea, and a California liberal Senator who's in the closet. Comedy and drama, and bold reform program for the criminal justice system results.

## VATICAN REHAB:
Rick and Ellen connect with a US member of the Belgian family of the Counts of Flanders that some believe is descended from Christ (a la Da Vinci Code). He seeks to take over the Vatican and use its wealth for alleviating problems of health and education. Rick and Ellen devise a takeover program using a massive fund in Switzerland that was established by the Vatican and Swiss after WW2 to covertly fight Communism. Conservatives in the

Vatican fight back. Rick enlists Saudi help
with Mideast peace plan involving the
Vatican paying reparations for the
Crusades. Many twists and turns.

## HOLLYWOOD REHAB:
Rick and Ellen at a Hollywood fundraiser
nearly shot as drug lords try to assassinate
California liberal Senator. Twin
Guatemalan priests, one in LA and one in
Guatemala, central to the drug trade, form
alliance with Venezuelans and Iranians to
use drug channels to smuggle suicide
vests and explosives into the USA. Rick
and Ellen enlist help from Hollywood
hooker who reforms and from a nun
working for Vatican intelligence who serves
illegal Mexican immigrants. Rick and the
Pope cooperate to take down corrupt
Mexican officials and drug lords and deliver
them to Guantanamo Bay on the Pope's
plane.
\*\*\*\*\*\*\*\*\*\*\*\*\*\*\*\*\*\*\*\*\*\*\*\*\*\*\*\*\*\*\*\*\*\*\*\*\*\*\*\*\*\*\*\*\*\*\*
\*\*\*\*\*\*\*\*\*\*\*\*\*\*\*\*\*\*\*\*\*\*\*\*\*\*\*\*\*\*\*\*\*\*\*\*\*\*\*\*\*\*\*\*\*\*\*
\*\*\*\*\*\*\*\*\*\*\*\*\*\*\*\*\*\*\*\*\*\*\*\*\*\*\*\*\*\*\*\*\*\*\*\*\*\*\*\*\*\*\*\*\*\*\*
\*\*


## JACQUELINE KENNEDY ONASSIS: The Imaginary Autobiography
Combines things the author knows to be true
from working with her, and inferences he made.
It assumes Jackie took a CIA job actually offered
to her in 1951 and kept it. The marriage to JFK is
arranged by the CIA unknown to him but known
to his father, Joe. She remained an agent all her
life, collaborated with the Russian spy of
Squished: Jackie Kennedy, Espionage, Murder
and Me, who was murdered by staged auto
accident in France.

## DOVER ROAD:
Poignant story based on a true
history of thirty-year-old scion of a
wealthy family in Santa Barbara, a
heroin addict who tries suicide

because he has hit the point that he can't stay alive and be hopeless. Theme of spiritual poverty in the midst of material plenty, and no one is a lost cause. Son realizes his father is an addict too, addicted to making money. Son's redemption opens father's eyes and saves him. Book skewers the wealthy of Santa Barbara.

## RUDOLPH THE PENGUIN
A selection of Children's bedtime stories about a penguin and his best friend, the Czar of Russia

Made in the USA
San Bernardino, CA
22 September 2018